Praise

'David's practical and innovative methodology, stemming from years of experience within education, is neatly packaged into this clear and concise book.

David truly understands parents' deepest challenges and brilliantly articulates solutions to resolving the most typical mistakes/problems parents face in mentoring their children.

If you are a parent looking to decipher the educational maze to maximise your child's full potential within education, this book will provide you with a fantastic guide and step-by-step process. I look forward to sharing this with our community of parents around the world.'

> – **Sebastian Bates**, founder of
> Warrior Academy

'David C. Hall writes from the heart and from deeply personal and professional experience. His passion for empowering children and inspiring every single child to greatness shines through every page. I found myself recognising the way I was parented and the effect it had on me as well as my own parenting style, how that is shaping my children along with areas where I could perhaps do more. It gave me real focus as my elder son transitions to high school this September. I love David's positive and inclusive philosophy, that "academic success does not discriminate" and that "every child, irrespective of their learning disposition and socioeconomic background" can achieve the greatness they were destined for. A genuinely thought-provoking book for any parent, educator or, indeed, anyone working with children.'

– **Sapna Pieroux**, founder of InnerVisions
ID Brand Consultancy

'Rarely do you find a book on raising resilient children that is well-researched and written, explains a substantive theory clearly, is based on sustained pragmatic frontline and industry experience…and comes from a place of impeccable values.'

– **Andrew Priestley**, leadership mentor

'As a mother of a daughter, *Inspire Your Child's Greatness* is exactly the book I needed to read. There were many times where I found myself nodding along in agreement – like with navigating the educational maze where I am often flummoxed by Year 4 maths. There are several questions and tools throughout the book which can be used immediately and with ease. The parenting principles are super useful and the section on balancing everything totally resonated as I have a demanding career and often question if I am good enough at home. The questions in this section allowed me a moment to reflect and realise that actually, I'm doing the best I can and that is good enough.'

– **Sophie Milliken**, founder of
Smart Resourcing Solutions

'*Inspire Your Child's Greatness* is a must-read for adults seeking guidance regarding their child's educational success. David C. Hall brings his own personal experience of difficulties in education, as well as his own academic expertise, to bear on the topic identified in the subtitle '7 Principles to Guide Young People from Struggle to Success'. This straightforward and fascinating read magnifies the challenges faced in education, and offers practical tools and strategies to overcome them, which can be easily implemented within the education and home settings. David C. Hall highlights the need for adults to both empower and enable children to follow their own unique paths in life, and that nothing is impossible, if they only believe. This read has reinforced the importance of having a well thought-out learning strategy, and the necessity of creating the appropriate environment that is conducive to each child's learning. I am sure that the reader will come away with a deepened understanding of how to specifically unlock their child's potential, overcome possible barriers in their way, and ensure each child is in the best possible position to flourish in life.'

– **Melissa Morrison,**
educational psychologist

'This book will benefit any parent, child or educator to become even better at how they think and therefore how they act. As the book makes clear, unlocking a child's potential is a collective responsibility and achievable for any child (however they may have been previously labelled). With my own work with adults in igniting their inner potential, I have seen time and again how adopting the right mindset can work wonders with the outcomes achieved. This book provides clear, step-by-step instructions on how we can do this for our children. The real test, as always, is in the application. If one were to apply even some of the principles outlined in this wonderful book, they will experience improvement in their achievements.'

> – **Kul Mahay**, CEO of Ignite Your
> Inner Potential

'This book is truly mind blowing! Each page offers new insights and practical information that is life-changing. Not only does it give you the best practices for how to develop our younger generation to fulfil their potential, but it also gives you the motivation and inspiration to become limitless in your own life. David is a great author and the concepts and methods in this book are game changing.'

> – **Cordell Jeffers**, award-winning
> changemaker, entrepreneur and speaker

'If you want to see a generation of young people making a Dent in the universe through their talents, this book is for you. David C. Hall will guide educators, parents and policy-makers though the *Inspire Your Child's Greatness* methodology that will inspire any child to live a fulfilled, successful and transformed life, and to have a passion-driven career and life.'

> – **Daniel Priestley**, co-founder of
> Dent Global

INSPIRE
YOUR CHILD'S
GREATNESS

7 Principles to Guide Young People
from Struggle to Success

DAVID C HALL

R^ethink

First published in Great Britain in 2021 by Rethink Press
(www.rethinkpress.com)

Cover image © Shutterstock | Debra Hughes

Contents

Foreword   1

Introduction   5

PART ONE   The Greatness Within   11

1 Your Child Is Destined For Greatness   13
   Three pillars of greatness   15
   Summary   18

2 The Challenges Parents Face   19
   Navigating the educational maze   20
   Work–life balance   22
   Purpose   24
   Benefits of finding your purpose   25
   Summary   29

3 The Challenges Children Face   31
   Adversity   31
   Learning challenges   33
   Key Stage transition and summer
   holiday regression   36

Summary   39

4   The Risks Of NEET   41
    Effects of NEET   43
    Contributing factors   45
    Reducing NEET   46
    Children with special educational needs   50
    Parental involvement   52
    Summary   53

PART TWO   Unlocking Your Child's Potential   55

5   Picture   57
    Fulfilment   59
    Personal leadership versus management   62
    Summary   63

6   Parent   65
    Connection   66
    Cultivation   68
    Parenting principles   70
    Free-for-all parenting   73
    Disempowering parenting   75
    Empowering parenting   78
    Summary   81

7   Programme   83
    Habits   84
    Sleep   87

Summary 90

8 **Partnership** **91**
Benefits of partnership 92
Triad Partnership Model 93
Parents 94
School 97
Other agencies and professionals 98
Summary 99

9 **Practice** **101**
Learning flow 103
Learning systems 105
Summary 110

10 **Passion** **113**
Why is passion important? 114
Finding your child's passion 116
Summary 117

11 **Path** **119**
The occupational and vocational paradigms 120
Purpose of education 122
Financial literacy and wealth 123
Summary 124

PART THREE From Struggle To Success **127**

12 **An Empowering Mindset** **129**
Building an empowering mindset 131

Belief and intelligence   132
Self-efficacy   133
Summary   137

13 An Effective Learning Strategy   139
Disempowering learning strategy   140
Empowering learning strategy   144
Summary   145

14 A Supportive Environment   147
Peer pressure   147
An empowering team   151
Summary   153

Conclusion   155

Acknowledgements   157

Resources   159
The Inspire Your Greatness Scorecard   159
The Inspire Your Greatness Seminar   159
Events   160

References   161

The Author   171

Foreword

When I came across David on Facebook, I was blown away to see someone who was using education not simply to help children pass their exams but to reach the greatness they had within. David's inspirational story and lived experience, from being a boy written off by the educational system to one who excelled in school against the odds, is one I was personally and truly motivated by. It's clear that for David, this book isn't just a collection of pages bound together; no, this is his purpose – to help parent and child along their journey of lifelong learning and greatness.

As the attainment gap between poor pupils and their peers in England widens at an alarming rate, we see these pupils average 18.1 months of learning behind their peers by the time they finish their GCSEs. This is the same gap as five years ago, whereas in primary schools the gap increased for the first time since 2007, up from 9.2 months in 2018 to 9.3 months a year later

(Education Policy Institutes' 'Education in England: Annual Report 2020').

This book you're about to read is game-changing in its approach to helping parents navigate their way through the maze of education that their children are walking through every day.

I have spent the last decade working with and teaching entrepreneurship to over 25,000 children and young people from 7 to 18 years old. We have won countless awards, been featured in media outlets across the world and have grown exponentially during the pandemic. We have seen firsthand the need for educational attainment and achievement that has become more critical than ever before.

In this book David shares examples of everyday children, with challenges we can all relate to, who have struggled to reach their full potential. He shows you the step-by-step systems and principles that he uses to overcome and overachieve in partnership with his students. But he doesn't stop there. David's experience and insight into child development widens to the family unit and how and why this is crucial to the academic potential of children. We know that a child's experience is whole so why should their learning be different?

At a time when education is against the ropes, and being challenged from early years to university, it's now that educators, parents and policymakers must do all we can to reinvigorate the spirit of education at its core. David's unique perspective and holistic approach to education makes this book special – very special.

I am fortunate to be part of the journey for David and his amazing organisation, Potential Unlocked, to help realise the greatness in every child. We will no longer accept the prevailing narrative that educational excellence is only for those who have. When you read this book, you'll too be empowered to not only believe but to know that your child with your support can do great things in their lives. That they can find their purpose in life and share that with the world.

Julian Hall
'The Ultrapreneur' and founder of Ultra Education

Introduction

Every parent wants their child to be happy, bright and successful. You believe that there is greatness in your child. You want to ignite the passion in your child so they can flourish, not only in the here and now, but also in the future. However, on the road to having happy, bright and successful children there are hurdles which can prevent this from becoming a reality.

Have you experienced a sticking point in igniting the greatness in your child? Is your child currently underachieving due to a glass ceiling that is preventing them from fulfilling their learning potential? Whatever the issue may be – dyslexia, attention deficit disorder (ADHD), dyspraxia, autism, mental health issues, gaps in knowledge, or behaviour challenges in the classroom environment or even in the home environment – whatever is causing your child to struggle, this book will home in on the root cause of that underachievement and help you to support your child to reach their full potential.

You may be concerned that your child is falling behind, or has already fallen behind, with their educational progress. Official support resources that could help you and your child may be lacking, and you could be worried that you lack the tools necessary to unlock the potential in your child and are failing as a parent.

Does all this sound familiar?

I am the founder of Potential Unlocked, whose mission is to train children and young people in their greatness to become fulfilled and successful, and transformed to have a passion-driven career and life.

My passion for seeing children flourish is due to my own personal story. At the age of three I was diagnosed with dyslexia, which meant that I was statemented, and a speech therapist was appointed to help me with a speech impediment. Reading was a massive challenge for me, as was spelling. Whenever I had to read aloud, I would mispronounce words, add words in and take words out – and be mocked by my peers. As a result, not only was I placed in the bottom set in all subjects, but I also struggled with confidence and self-esteem.

At the end of Year 4, it was agreed that I would be integrated back into mainstream education for Year 5, to raise my academic profile. However, at the end of Year 6 I attained only a Level 2 in my SATS – putting me four years behind my peers. Starting secondary school, I was told by my form tutor that I would not be top of the class but, encouraged by my parents, I was determined to be among the high attainers.

Four years later, thanks to my parents' support and developing an effective learning strategy, a supportive environment and empowering mindset enabled me to overcome the barriers to my learning and gave me the confidence to set and achieve goals. I left secondary school with ten GCSE passes at grades A* to C – among the highest scores in my year.

My experience convinced me that every child, irrespective of their background and learning disposition, can achieve academic success and realising their goals in life; that in every child there is potential greatness; and that any child's life can be transformed by applying the right strategies for learning and development. I set up Potential Unlocked in 2017 as a training centre where children, young people and adults can flourish in their greatness to have fulfilled, successful and transformed lives, and to lead passion-driven careers making an impact in the world through their gifts and talents. Potential Unlocked has since helped unlock countless children and young people and adults to their potential to achieve greatness.

This book is based on thirteen years' experience in education, during which I've worked as a teaching assistant, science teacher, learning consultant, learning coach and tutor. I've also provided advocacy and support to parents, educators and local authorities.

From this experience, I developed seven principles that
will unlock potential in children and young people,
empower them to break through their glass ceiling,
build a fulfilling career and enrich their lives. These
principles are outlined in this book, alongside case
studies of children who have achieved their potential
through working with Potential Unlocked. This book
will show you how to identify your child's potential
greatness and unlock that potential, empowering them
to achieve greatness.

Inspire Your Child's Greatness will guide you through this
process in three stages. Part One will show you that
your child is destined for greatness, which they can
achieve irrespective of any glass ceiling limiting their
potential. You will also gain insights into the societal
challenges that you and your child might face, such as
employability. Part One also examines the challenges
parents experience – challenges that can contribute
to your child underachieving. Finally, it will provide
insights into the daily challenges children themselves
can face and the practical strategies that can be put
in place to enable them to overcome these challenges.

Part Two shows you how to unlock your child's
potential and inspire their greatness using the unique
seven-step Inspire Your Child's Greatness methodology,
which will give you all the tools you need. It demon-
strates how you can help your child build the right
picture in their mind's eye – a picture of success – and
how to create an empowering environment, which is

essential to unlocking their potential. You will learn how to build a programme of habits and routines that will sustain your child's progress and success; how to develop learning practices that will lead to academic success; how to establish the right partnerships to leverage the potential in your child; how to identify passion in your child; and finally, how to identify the path that will lead your child to financial literacy – not only by following a career that they are passionate about, but also by building intergenerational wealth.

Part Three will consolidate the information provided in the first two parts to outline the three keys that will unlock your child's potential: an empowering mindset, an effective learning strategy and a positive, supportive environment.

Inspire Your Child's Greatness is your pathway to overcoming the obstacles in the way of your child achieving success in life. What can be more important than that?

PART ONE
THE GREATNESS WITHIN

The child in your care is destined for greatness, irrespective of their learning disposition; irrespective of the path that they have started on; irrespective of the challenges that you yourself face. Your child has greatness invested in them whether they are in mainstream education, attend a Pupil Referral Unit (PRU), or have an education, health and care (EHC) plan, or demonstrate traits of neurodiversity or emotional challenges – in short, whatever their situation. And, whether you are a parent/guardian, educator or policymaker, you play a vital role. More than this, you have a responsibility to create an environment in which you can unlock potential. In the first part of this book, we will look at how you can identify the greatness invested in your child.

1

Your Child Is Destined For Greatness

What do we understand by the term 'greatness'? How we define greatness ultimately determines how we perceive greatness and how we unlock the greatness in our child. Some people measure greatness by the accumulation of wealth, by the success symbols of cars and houses. These symbols are not the true measure of greatness and the danger of pursuing them is that we do not feel fulfilled in what we are doing. What is the use in attaining these things if we lose our soul?

I encourage you to reconsider the definition of greatness, to consider its true essence, which is associated with character development and service. Values such

as integrity, honesty and building strong relationships
are timeless and universal. We are all drawn to people
who display good character, who have integrity, who
are honest, forbearing, long suffering. These are all
attributes of a strong character and lay the foundation
for success in life. Character development is the foundation of greatness. With this definition in mind, the
question arises: what opportunities have you given to
your child, or the child in your care, to develop their
character? How are you supporting them to develop
resilience, emotional intelligence and kindness? Think
of a restaurant. In any restaurant there is a waiter,
whose role it is to ensure that the guests' needs are
being met, to be of service to them and ensure that
they have a great experience. The waiter understands
that their job is to serve their clients. In a similar way,
the true essence of greatness is to use one's gifts and
talents to serve the world, making an impact.

Character development leads to good work ethic,
which is a necessity if you are to develop a craft. But
service is outward facing. Your gifts and talents are
not for you, but for the world to benefit from. The
essence of greatness is being aware of your gifts and
talents, understanding how they can be utilised to
serve the world and make a difference, and leaving a
generational legacy.

Three pillars of greatness

Greatness has three essential characteristics, three pillars: legacy, direction and passion. Let's look at each of these in turn.

Pillar One: Legacy

The mindset of an individual who embodies greatness is to think in terms of generational impact. They think long term, of the generations to come. They understand that greatness involves some sacrifice in terms of today's needs in order to meet those of tomorrow. They see the bigger picture, not simply the now. They understand that to be great, and to grow in greatness, requires a mindset of service. Legacy is their paradigm of greatness, not status in the present.

What legacy are you leaving right now? None of us wants to think about dying, but just for a moment, ask yourself: what would you like to be said about you at your funeral? Are you already on a path to leaving a legacy? By the same token, how are you supporting the child or children in your care in order to leave a legacy for them, and to facilitate them in leaving their own legacy? There is no 'I' or 'me' in team, and greatness is a team sport, where it is necessary to work together, to drive that legacy of greatness across the generations.

Pillar Two: Direction

When you are in greatness, there is a clear sense of direction to your life. Ultimately, leadership hinges on knowing what you were born to do, what your purpose is. A visionary leader can execute a plan based on their purpose. Your vision, when aligned to your purpose, gives you direction. Once you are going in a clear direction, aligned with your purpose, you can lead.

What direction are you going in today? Is it aligned to your purpose? Too often, we chase the cars, the house and the money, the success symbols, but this is not aligned to our purpose. Your purpose gives you life, energises you, gives you a sense of happiness, of fulfilment; chasing 'things' leads only to a void. Which are you pursuing: things, or your true purpose?

Instead of 'things', pursue your gift and talents – this will create opportunities for you. Your gift will bring you before great people and will bring the right people into your life, enable you to collaborate, to increase your impact and influence, strengthen your leadership and broaden your legacy. Money follows influence and impact, not the other way around. Money follows service. It is important to understand this.

What influence do you have today? How are you shaping your child to grow in leadership skills, to enable them to exert influence? Are they influencing change in ideas and feelings, reacting in a positive way to negative peer pressure, leading their generation; or are they being led, passive?

Pillar Three: Passion

Much of our validation is sought externally, when we seek approval from others. We measure ourselves against media images, try to conform to stereotypes, to be 'normal'. Instead, we should look inside ourselves and find where our passion lies. We should live 'inside-out'. We want to create a generation of young adults who are driven by passion; who understand that gifts and talents are intrinsically linked to passion; who ask, 'How can I serve? How can I have an impact? How can I grow my influence to have an even greater impact?' When we live inside-out, we are no longer in competition, we are no longer trying to be better than others. If you are in business, you are no longer competing against another business in a similar industry. The only competition is with yourself, to grow in your gift and use your talents to have an impact.

Today is your opportunity to recognise and explore your child's passion. What is it that will drive your child to achieve greatness?

Summary

Every child has the potential for greatness, meaning your child has greatness within them that you can help to unlock. Greatness is not what many assume it to be; it involves living inside-out and is intrinsically linked to the development of good character and a strong work ethic. True greatness is founded on three pillars: legacy, direction and passion. As parents, educators and policymakers we have a duty, a responsibility to create a movement of young people who are driven by their passion to make a difference to others, to create a legacy and to walk in their greatness. Inspire the greatness in your child today.

2

The Challenges
Parents Face

In trying to unlock a child's potential and bring out their greatness, parents can and will encounter various challenges. From my work and experience, I've found that these challenges tend to fall into three broad categories: navigating the educational maze; achieving a work–life balance that enables you to both inspire and support your child; and finding and understanding your own purpose – which, when achieved, makes a work–life balance easier to realise.

Navigating the educational maze

Having worked with both parents and children in
a variety of learning environments, I have noticed a
recurring theme, what I refer to as difficulty 'navigating the educational maze'. A maze is defined as:
'a complex system of passages or paths...designed
to confuse people who try to find their way through
it.'[1] The word education derives from the Latin 'to
draw out'. Combining the two terms, an educational
maze is, metaphorically speaking, a path strewn with
challenges to drawing out the potential in your child
(or, if you are an educator or policymaker, the children
under your care). This is the cause of much frustration,
typically due to a lack of knowledge. Arming yourself
with knowledge from reliable sources will give you the
wisdom needed to navigate the educational maze with
poise, confidence, calmness and a winner's mindset.

As a parent, have you been in the situation where your
child comes home from school with homework to do
by a set date? You put aside time to support them
and you begin to show them the method you were
taught at school – only for your child to tell you that
the method you use is wrong? Then you try to use the
method they have been taught at school, without fully
understanding it yourself, with the result that your
child is confused, having been shown two different
methods. Has this happened to you? Or a more general
example: your child has SATs or GCSEs to revise for,
and you think, 'How in the world do I support my
child in preparing for their exams? How did I revise

effectively? Is this the best way for my child?' Has this happened to you?

If either of these experiences sounds familiar, you have found yourself in an educational maze.

The way out of this maze is often hard to discern. Perhaps you receive communications from the school to which you don't know how to respond. Maybe you attend meetings at the school but don't know what questions to ask. Are you frustrated by these challenges? Are you tired of going round and round in circles? Do you feel guilty for not knowing how to navigate the educational maze?

It doesn't have to stay this way. There is a way out. An ancient Chinese proverb advises that, 'The person who removes a mountain begins by carrying away small stones.' The mountain is symbolic of the overwhelm of challenges you face – but if you tackle them 'stone by stone', you can overcome them.

Some practical ideas for how to navigate the educational maze are to:

1. Get acquainted with the national curriculum and the milestones of each Key Stage.
2. Attend parents' evenings with questions prepared beforehand.
3. Seek out a learning coach or learning consultant who can empower you and your child to navigate the educational maze with confidence, assurance and wisdom.

Work-life balance

Many parents face a permanent challenge in balancing the demands of work with the demands of their home environment and life in general. The 2007 British Social Attitudes Report concluded that 58% of women and 69% of men felt their career demands interfered with their family life,[2] and a study by Rutgers University and the University of Connecticut found that 90% of working adults felt they did not spend as much time as they wanted to with their families.[3]

Work–life balance is defined as: 'A state of equilibrium in which the demands of both a person's job and personal life are equal.'[4] The ability to function to a high standard in a work environment while enjoying quality time with children in a home environment is truly a balancing act. Take the opportunity to raise your children to be emotionally resilient and to live successful lives. It is easier to spend time with your children while they're young and nurture them, so that, in years to come, you are not spending a lifetime repairing broken adults.

In considering your own balancing act, ask yourself the following questions:

- Do you attend your child's parents' evenings?
- Have you ever seen your child perform in extracurricular activities?

- When you finish your day's work, have you got the capacity to meet your child's spiritual, physical, emotional and intellectual needs?

If you answered no to any of these questions, take another moment to reflect on your life as it is now and answer some further questions:

- In perfect conditions, what would your life look like?
- What are the key areas of your life?
- What is at the centre of your life?

The key components of your life right now may be family, finances, work, friends, social life, spouse, hobbies, your health. All of these are essential. Now consider the centre of your life. Some people place work at the centre of their life, which makes it unbalanced, as will be discussed below. For a balanced and meaningful life, at the centre, or the heart, should be your life purpose. This will give meaning to and direct every area of your life. If you feel that you have not got the work–life balance that you and your child(ren) deserve, you could seek out a learning or life coach who can help you bring your work and life together again by identifying your purpose.

Purpose

Purpose is a much talked-about topic, and it is common to ask oneself, 'What is my purpose? What is the meaning of my life?' Some people put work at the centre of their lives, seeing their work as the purpose of their life. Yet it is a sad fact that 90% of the world's workforce do not like their job.[5] This means only 10% of workers enjoy what they do for a living and could reasonably consider it their life purpose.

This takes on great significance when you understand that the average adult in full-time employment will typically spend one-third of their waking hours at work. If you are employed five days a week for forty-eight weeks per year from the age of eighteen until you retire at sixty-five, you will spend more than 70,000 hours – or eight years of your life – at work. That is a lot of time to spend doing something you do not enjoy, something that is not aligned to your purpose. In fact, one of the main reasons why 90% of the workforce don't enjoy what they do for a living is precisely because there is a misalignment between their life purpose and their vocation. They are in an occupational paradigm.

In an ideal scenario, you don't want to be part of that 90%, but instead find absolute fulfilment in your work. To achieve this, your work should be aligned to your life purpose, as should your choice in spouse and the way you manage and utilise your finances. All these things should be in synergy; everything should revolve around your life purpose. As we saw in Chapter 1, walking in greatness requires living inside-out rather than outside-in. When you are living inside-out, and you are in a vocation paradigm, the work that you do does not *feel* like work.

You have purpose inside of you, take the first step today. Believing that you have purpose is the first step to greatness. The second step will then emerge, followed by the third and so on. If you are not aware of your life purpose and feel that you are living below your potential, this does not have to continue. There is a way out. You deserve to be happy, to be content and to feel that your work is adding value to society. You deserve a lifestyle where you can perform at work to a high level and still have the capacity to support your children at home. It is therefore essential to be aware of your gifts and talents and find a meaningful way to express those through serving others. What are you naturally good at? Think of things you do where time goes quickly, where you are 'in your flow'. These are indicators of your purpose.

Benefits of finding your purpose

There are various reasons why it is essential that you identify or find a life purpose, and many studies have highlighted the benefits of a purpose-driven life.[6,7,8,9,10] These include:

Energy

Purpose-driven individuals are likely to be energised because they are living in their 'flow' state, achieved by tapping into their gifts and talents. In this energetic state, you find meaning in your day-to-day work. In your home environment with your children, you feel more energised and happier because from nine to five, you are doing what you were born to do. You are walking in your personal greatness.

Resilience

Purpose-driven individuals are more resilient and less prone to anxiety, boredom and frustration because they are on a mission to make a difference through what is dear to their heart, through their gifts and talents. Studies have shown that those who lack purpose in their life are susceptible to depression, anxiety and stress and have a greater likelihood of developing damaging habits such as substance abuse, whether that's alcohol or drugs.[11] Even worse, individuals who are self-absorbed or lack a 'mission' in their life are more vulnerable to suicide as they are more driven by their own needs.[12]

Positive work ethic

As we discussed in Chapter 1, good character development is based on values such as integrity, ethical behaviour and honesty. It should be a daily pursuit to work on developing our character and being a trustworthy person. This will feed into a positive work ethic and you will be so absorbed in making a difference that work will become stress-free.

Motivation

Finding your purpose allows you to be a 'giver', not a 'taker', serving others through your gifts and talents. The more these gifts and talents have been harnessed and honed, the greater the quality of service you can provide, making more of an impact. This will give you greater intrinsic motivation, meaning you wake up in the morning with a spring in your step because you are doing something you are passionate about and that you have been called to do.

Optimism

When you are living with purpose, you will be more upbeat. When your alarm goes off on a Monday morning, you will be happy to go to work, knowing that you are going to make an impact. And on Friday afternoon, you are looking forward to the weekend and enjoying family time, but also looking forward to Monday, when you can make even more of an impact through your purpose.

Self-esteem

People with purpose have greater self-esteem. You no longer see yourself as being in competition with others. You understand that you are one part of a puzzle and are more open to collaboration. You measure your progress in relation to your purpose, not in relation to your peers, or what others think of you. You no longer seek external validation; you are validated by your purpose.

Direction

Purpose means that there is a clear direction for your life; that your decisions are made in alignment with your life purpose and in accordance with timeless principles and goals. This gives you a moral compass with which to navigate life in accordance with your values.

Sense of fulfilment and life satisfaction

Purpose-driven individuals gain a sense of fulfilment because they are serving the world through their gifts and talents. There is something special about finding meaning, in living a life where every day is the best day of your life, where you are content and fulfilled. Purpose gives meaning to every area of your life: your finances, your relationships, your vocation, your network. It is the hub at which all parts of your life meet. It gives you stability. It gives you inner strength and satisfaction.

Flow

Have you ever had a job where you are constantly watching the clock and counting down to home time? Have you ever spent months counting down to your next holiday? This is a strong indicator that you are not in your flow, and certainly not in a vocational paradigm (discussed in Chapter 11).

Being in flow (what some describe as being 'in the zone') is when you are so absorbed in the moment that your awareness of your surroundings is minimal and you lose track of time. When you are in a work situation, ask yourself: does time go quickly for you or are you constantly watching the clock? Once you find your flow, you will become happier, feel more energised, and time will no longer be of the essence.

Summary

Parents trying to unlock the potential in their child and set them on the path to greatness may encounter various challenges, across three main areas: navigating the educational maze, achieving a work–life balance and identifying their own life purpose. The education system your child is learning within is likely quite different to the one you experienced; you can find a way through the educational maze by arming yourself with knowledge of the school and curriculum so that you can identify the best ways of supporting your child.

As a parent, identifying your own purpose and walking in your own greatness is a crucial first step to being able to inspire and support your child in doing the same. When you know your purpose and your work and life are in alignment with it, a work–life balance is easier to achieve: you can enjoy a purpose-driven career, while at the same time being able to meet the needs of your child. Other benefits of finding your purpose and living in alignment with it are greater energy and resilience; a positive work ethic; more motivation, optimism and higher self-esteem; a clear direction and moral compass for your life; a sense of fulfilment and life satisfaction; and a life lived in flow, where you're never watching the clock and wishing time away. All of these things put you in the strongest possible position to guide your child to building a life where they can enjoy the same.

Be part of a movement of parents, educators and poli-cymakers who are purpose-driven, who have made the decision to stand up and to be counted. It is no longer acceptable to blend in with others. It is your time to do what you are here for. You are good enough. Even though you may make mistakes, your child can benefit from your story, your expertise, your gift, your talent.

3

The Challenges Children Face

It is not only parents who will face challenges in unlocking their child's potential. Children also face many and various challenges throughout their journey through education and into adulthood. If they are to rise to these challenges and walk in their greatness, they must be prepared and able to overcome adversity.

Adversity

Many successful people have flourished from adversity, with their success emerging out of obscurity. Adversity is designed to elevate you to your next level of greatness.

I use the analogy of a diamond. A diamond is a commodity of great beauty, but it was not always that way. Diamonds take billions of years to form and their formation requires heat and pressure – adversity. Even once they have been taken out of the ground, they must be chipped and polished to perfection. The same applies to greatness, which is the result of overcoming extreme pressure and challenges.

It's important to realise that these challenges are not all negative, nor were they sent to destroy you. On the contrary, they serve to form your character, to enable you to develop your greatness. Inside us all are gifts and talents, but sometimes they are not fully realised until we are presented with a situation that brings them into the light and sharpens them until they shine. It is important that your child understands this so that they can rise to rather than shy away from the challenges they face.

From age ten, I wanted to be a pharmacist. I wanted this because it paid well and because it would give me social status and the lifestyle that I coveted. In other words, I wanted it for all the wrong reasons. This was the start of my diamond journey; there were challenges to come. A degree that should have taken three years to complete, took me six. My father was unwell and had to be hospitalised, so I had to work to support myself and study at the same time. Yet I had time for introspection. This period enabled me to press the pause button and to evaluate what my purpose was. I asked myself the question: 'What could I do daily that will enable me to be paid and still be fulfilled?'

The answer that came to me was to unlock potential in children, young people and adults. I knew that it would be a challenge, but if I had not faced and overcome that challenge, I would never have unlocked my own potential. Every challenge your child goes through is designed to unlock their greatness.

Has your child been through, or are they currently experiencing, adversity? What can they learn from it? Think about your own story, the challenges you have faced in your life, and how this could encourage and inspire another generation to achieve their own greatness. You should embrace your story unapologetically and use it to liberate your child, helping them to find their purpose and passion in life.

Learning challenges

Learning is the ability to process information and turn it into knowledge and skill, which can result in a transformation of behaviour, action and habits. We all have a unique 'learning flow', which relates to our ability to not only understand new information, but also to apply it to new situations and circumstances. Challenges arise when we are taught information that is not aligned to our learning flow; this can cause frustration, a poor self-image, poor self-esteem and,

notably, underachievement. Alternatively, this misalignment can be a result of undiagnosed learning
difficulties, such as dyslexia, dyscalculia, dysgraphia,
autism or ADHD. Furthermore, trauma or Adverse
Child Experiences (ACEs) are notoriously known to
hinder academic progress if left unchecked.

We know that there is a clear relationship between
children with special educational needs (SEN) and
school exclusion, as these children are likely to display
behavioural challenges to mask the frustration or anxiety they experience when required to learn within the
standard education system. Children's self-concept (the
way they see themselves) is influenced by their past
academic performance. I believe that in SEN students,
facing repeated academic challenges and/or receiving
grades that don't reflect their potential, their self-image
is further lowered, massively impacting their confidence.[13] This sets them off on a downward spiral of
low intrinsic motivation and low attainment, since
motivation is critical for academic success.[14] This can
lead to the child 'failing' in their education or training
and becoming NEET (not in education, employment
or training) – this will be discussed in detail in the next
chapter.

It is, therefore, imperative that we recognise when
children have a learning difficulty and realise that
this 'difficulty' is in fact a gift – it is the pressure, the
challenge that can enable them to achieve greatness, to
become a diamond. Too often, children with learning

difficulties are simply labelled as 'stupid' by those around them.

Richard Branson is dyslexic, but this has not prevented his success. In fact, many successful entrepreneurs are dyslexic. People with ADHD are known for their attention to detail. Those with autism often have phenomenal recall and organisational skills. The key when dealing with any of these 'conditions' is to understand the child's learning flow, so that they can be enabled to learn effectively. As a parent it is essential to never, ever convey to your child that they are at a disadvantage. Instead, explain to them that they are beautifully made, like a diamond, and that they will have a bright and sparkling future, just like any other child. When you have these expectations for your child, and then you nurture them, they will flourish and achieve greatness.

Perhaps the most famous scientist and mathematician in history, Albert Einstein, had several interesting characteristics. For one, he had trouble socialising, especially as an adult. As a child, he experienced severe speech delays and later echolalia, or the habit of repeating sentences to himself.[15] And of course, Einstein was incredibly technically minded. These characteristics have led experts to consider that he could be placed somewhere on the autism spectrum.

Key Stage transition and summer holiday regression

The British education system is structured according to what are called Key Stages. These denote particular 'stages' of learning development that should be achieved by a certain age. There are five Key Stages: the Early Years Foundation Stage (EYFS) covers the years up to the age of five; Key Stage 1 covers learning between the ages of five and seven and includes Year 1 and Year 2 of the school structure; Key Stage 2 is subdivided into Lower Key Stage 2, which is Year 3 and Year 4, and Upper Key Stage 2, which is Years 5 and 6; then, once children reach secondary education, come Key Stage 3 (Years 7 to 9) and Key Stage 4 (Years 10 and 11). This means that what we call the 'Key Stage transitions', times where children are particularly vulnerable to learning challenges and regression, occur at the ages of around five, seven, eleven and fourteen.

In addition to the inherent challenges of these major transitions, something that can adversely affect children's learning and cause them to regress in their Key Stage progress is 'summer learning loss' (sometimes referred to as the 'summer slide' or 'summer setback'). It has been shown that working class children and those living in poverty tend to suffer from this phenomenon to a greater extent; summer losses range from regressions of one to two months in reading and up to three months of schoolyear learning in maths.[16]

Strategies to mitigate Key Stage regression

It has been observed that children's intrinsic motivation drastically changes as they journey through the educational system and, for some children, the ever-greater demands and higher expectations lead to a downward spiral of underachievement.[17] To optimise your child's progress, it is imperative to develop a learning strategy that will help them through these transitions and minimise summer holiday regression. This can be achieved through extra classes during term time and a (relaxed) routine of study during the summer holidays to consolidate basic knowledge in the core subjects and maintain recall of information. This will ensure continued progress in the new school year.

Since emotional wellbeing is linked to educational attainment, it is necessary to ensure that your child feels comfortable in each new phase of their education. It is common, for example, for children in Year 6 to find the transition to secondary school daunting. However, most secondary schools have a 'taster day', when your child can view the school, meet the staff and ask questions. These are also important for you as a parent or educator. Then, while the school itself may not change, in the transition from Key Stage 3 to Key Stage 4, there is a change of emphasis and learning style, with greater emphasis on assessment and increased pressure on children to manage their own time.

Learning flow

We talked in the last chapter about flow, in the context of work, but it also applies to learning.[18] When you are in a 'learning flow', you lose awareness of your surroundings and track of time. You can seamlessly process information and turn it into skill and knowledge, which as we know is what defines learning. It is the lack of learning flow that prevents some children from achieving in a school environment, specifically from doing well in tests, assessments and exams. The following case study illustrates this point.

CHRISTINE

Christine (not her real name) went to an established private school in Birmingham, UK. Christine was a diligent student. She would revise for hours and hours, and her parents were incredibly supportive. And yet Christine was not getting the grades that she deserved in her exams. She felt pressured, frustrated and demotivated, and believed that she would not achieve the grades needed to pursue her dream career.

We worked with her parents to establish a routine that would support her to achieve a Grade B in science, which she desperately wanted, and in partnership with her school to understand the curriculum structure and delivery. We developed some learning strategies around retention of knowledge and exam techniques that would be aligned with her learning flow and thereby improve her confidence and build an intrinsic motivation to achieve. We identified Christine's passion, what she loved to do, and mapped out a career plan that would help her to achieve her goals.

Christine achieved a Grade B in science. She was overjoyed and so were her parents.

Does Christine's situation sound familiar? Is your child trying to succeed, but the more they try, the lower their grades? Do you feel that their academic 'achievement' is not a true reflection of their ability? Is your child experiencing behavioural challenges at school? Are you tired of hearing reports that your child could do better, but are not sure how to support them so that they not only survive, but flourish in an education environment?

Being dyslexic myself, I was more or less written off at school. I had low self-esteem and confidence, but in my five-year secondary career I was able to achieve five grades above my expected grade. The system I'll show you in Part Two of this book is what I used personally, and what I use with my students.

Summary

Children face many challenges on their journey through education and into life as a young adult. At some point they will likely need to overcome adversity and learn to grow from it. They may encounter specific learning challenges that threaten their self-concept; they may struggle with their transition through the Key Stages; they could regress over the summer holidays; they may struggle to find their learning flow. These challenges, if they are not equipped and supported to overcome them, could limit your child's achievement potential and risk them becoming NEET.

It may be that your child is sitting under a glass ceiling, which they can perceive but are unable to break. You have an important role to play in supporting your child to break through the glass ceiling of underachievement so that they can climb the stairs to success – to a passionate, purpose-driven career and to a happy and successful life. In Part Two, you will learn some strategies and techniques that you can put in place to achieve this.

4

The Risks Of NEET

'NEET' are young people (those aged between 16 and 24) who are 'not in education, employment or training'. The end goal of parents, policymakers and educators is to empower children and young people to access either employment, entrepreneurship, education or training, by giving them the tools necessary to do so. Our dream is for them to have a career that they are passionate about and that will enable them to live a fulfilled, balanced life walking in their greatness.

The difference between education and training is that education is acquiring knowledge through teaching, whereas training involves learning a particular skill. Education tends to be based in a sixth-form college or university, whereas training is often 'on the job'. The aim of training is to improve an ability – learning by doing – whereas education aims to impart information through teaching, to build a knowledge base.

Our duty is to ensure that young people can develop the skillset needed to obtain a career, through employment or entrepreneurship, or obtain the credentials necessary to access a training or education programme, to fulfil their potential and walk in their greatness. As we know, all children are destined for greatness. Whether you are a parent, educator or policymaker, it is your innate desire to see children progress and do well in life; to not only survive, but to flourish, at whatever they put their hands to. We play an integral role as facilitators of that transformation and social mobilisation.

It has been shown that half of British children obtain five or more Grade 5–9 GCSEs,[19] including English, maths and sciences, which function as a passport to the next step in life's journey, whether that's further education (ie college/university), training (eg apprenticeships) or employment. Yet 36% of children do not obtain five or more Grade 5–9 GCSEs, meaning that one in three children cannot progress to further education, training or employment. This proves to be a major barrier to their progress in life.

Other data indicates that 11.1% of young people are not in education, employment or training, which equates to 765,000 young people in the UK.[20] This is a major concern for educators and parents, who have a duty to work together to reduce this number so that we can see more of our young people engaged in education and training programmes, enabling them to fulfil their purpose and be contributors to society, not takers from it.

It has been estimated that 16–18-year-olds who are NEET will cost society £56,000 each in their lifetimes[21] and that 20–24-year-olds who are not in employment cost society £22 million per week in Jobseeker's Allowance.[22] This presents various social challenges.

Effects of NEET

The impact of our youth not engaging in employment, education or training has several detrimental effects across different aspects of social life.

Poverty

Not being engaged in employment is the basis for poverty. The average pay for a full-time employee is £31,461 per annum.[23] The Household Below Average Income (HBAI) statistics identify poverty as being the condition when household income is 60% below the median.[24] This means that a household income of below £18,876 is deemed as poverty.

Poor physical and mental health

Those living in poverty and young people who are NEET are likely to experience poor physical health.

This effect is compounded: the longer they are NEET, the worse their physical health may become.

Being NEET also has a detrimental impact on young people's mental health. It increases their likelihood of depression, compared with their peers who are in education, employment or training. In fact, research has demonstrated that young men who are NEET are three times more likely to suffer from depression than their peers.[25] This is particularly concerning when you consider that depression can lead to suicidal thoughts and, sadly, suicide.

Crime

Youth who are NEET are more likely to commit a crime, due to the need to generate an income that would otherwise have been provided through employment or financial support while in education. In fact, it has been established that young men who are not in education, employment or training are four times more likely to engage in criminal activity that leads to a criminal record than their non-NEET peers.[26]

Alcoholism

It has been shown that 11% of sixteen to twenty-five-year-olds who are classed as NEET abuse alcohol; conversely, working to reduce the number of NEET young people has been shown to reduce incidences of alcoholism.[27]

Contributing factors

Several factors have been identified as contributing to the likelihood of children going on to become NEET as young adults.

Socioeconomic status

The socioeconomic status of parents is known to be a determining factor in young people becoming NEET.[28] It has been reported that 4.3 million children are raised in poverty and that this has massive ramifications for their future, with an increased likelihood of becoming NEET and a weakened prospect of high academic achievement.[29] Data also suggests that more socioeconomically deprived areas have a higher proportion of young people who are NEET.[30]

By contrast, children in socioeconomically privileged families are likely to be in full-time education both at age 16 and 18 and are subsequently likely to engage in employment.

GCSE results

Research has identified that GCSE results are also a strong indicator of becoming a NEET – even more so than socioeconomic status.[31] It has been documented that low levels of attainment in maths and English in particular are key indicators that a child or young person will become NEET.[32]

Reducing NEET

As parents, educators and policymakers, we should work collaboratively and strategically in our respective spheres of influence to reduce the number of NEETs in society. To achieve this, we need a clear focus and strategy. The government has already taken the initiative of extending compulsory full-time education from age sixteen to age eighteen, which means that all young people must continue in education or training until at least the age of 18. Beyond such policy changes, our role is to help to create a shared belief that every person has a purpose and can be a positive contributor to society, and to work to ensure that they are able to access education, employment or training as a vehicle for self-actualisation.

Some of the specific areas where the contributing factors to a child going on to become NEET can be addressed are:

Formative education

It is critical that children and young people benefit from a positive formative education (from age 4 to 18), through which they are empowered with the resources, skills and knowledge to flourish within an educational environment. It is common in educational institutions for children to be taught *what* to learn, but they are not necessarily taught *how* to learn. The *what* is knowledge, but the *how* is a skill. We need all children to be able to learn effectively.

Attendance

A child's school attendance rate and their academic attainment go hand in hand. Conversely, children who have poor attendance are more likely to under-achieve academically, as they will have gaps in their knowledge and find it increasingly difficult to catch up, which in turn can negatively affect their confidence and attainment. This sets the precedent for negative reinforcement of the belief that they are not intelligent.

Working to improve a child's attendance at school, with the right support in place, will improve their attainment level. It is like building a house. Would you build a house with no foundation? No. You would first lay the foundation and then build on top of it. The same principle applies to learning. The foundation of future learning is basic knowledge; without basic knowledge, it is difficult to build the further, more complex knowl-edge that is needed for academic success.

According to statutory guidance, UK schools are open for 190 days per year, from September to July. Children must be in attendance 180.5 days per school year; this is 95% of the total number of open days and is considered a 'good' attendance level. Research has demonstrated that 73% of children who achieve 95% school attendance achieve five or more GCSEs at Grades 4–9.[33] Other research suggests that children with 100% attendance are 2.2 times more likely to achieve five or more grades 4–9 at GCSE, including English and maths.[34]

By contrast, an attendance level of 90% or below, which is categorised as Persistent Absence (PA), has been shown to have a detrimental effect on academic attainment. For example, children with 50% school attendance have only a 3% chance of achieving five or more GCSEs at Grades 4–9.[35] Therefore, children with Persistent Absence (PA) are more likely to achieve lower grades in English and maths, due to poor attendance. Since the next step, post-16 education, requires GCSEs, it becomes difficult for these children to access, as do training programmes. This can start the young person off down a spiral to becoming NEET. One positive development, though, is that in recent years some training providers have allowed young people who do not have the required English and maths GCSEs to attain a Level 2 equivalent qualification through an apprenticeship or training programme.

Clearly, it is important that parents, policymakers and educators work as a collective, to increase the school attendance rate of children so that they can avoid falling into the NEET trap. We need to break the cycle and help facilitate social mobilisation for our young people.

School exclusion

A UK government report found that 7,894 children were permanently excluded from formal education (Reception to Year 11) in the academic year 2017/2018, and each day, an average of 2,000 pupils were excluded for a fixed period.[36] Exclusion from school has a significant impact on children's learning, making them vulnerable to continued underachievement and at increased risk of becoming NEET in the future. The exclusion rate is linked to several factors, including socioeconomic status, parents' special educational needs, mental health, and home environment. It has also been identified that children from specific ethnic groups are at higher risk of being excluded from school; these include Black Caribbean pupils, White Gypsy and Roma children and travellers of Irish heritage.[37]

Gender is also a factor: boys are far more likely to be permanently excluded from school than girls, with 89% of those permanently excluded and 87% of those excluded for a fixed period in primary education being boys. This may be explained by the fact that boys tend to show their dislike of education in a more outward way, through verbal demonstrations and physical violence, while girls will normally internalise their feelings.[38] This means that boys are more likely to display behavioural challenges (which is why they are more often excluded) while for girls the challenges are more often emotional, such as anxiety and depression.[39] It is imperative that we understand the different ways in which boys and girls tend to manifest their frustrations. When a child feels disempowered by an education system that requires them to learn in a specific way, for example using a learning strategy that is misaligned with their learning flow, this will result in frustration. These children haven't been taught how to learn effectively.

Children with special educational needs

Some young people underachieve within the school environment (and so run the risk of becoming NEET) because they have unidentified special educational needs (SEN) and are not getting the support they need. Generally, the mechanisms for identifying autism, dyslexia, ADHD, etc are inadequate, so that these children are liable to be excluded from education.[40] If behavioural challenges are a direct result of their learning disposition, they also run the risk of becoming NEET.

Again, boys are more likely to have SEN than girls[41] and, sadly, children with SEN are more likely to be excluded from school:[42] 45% of children excluded from formal education are believed to have SEN.[43] Children with SEN are also likely to suffer from a poor self-concept, reinforced through experiences of learning difficulties, which weaken their self-belief and 'label' them as 'not good enough' for academic success – or success in other areas of life.

More effort is required to educate parents so that they can quickly identify children's learning needs and obtain the support needed for them to flourish academically. More also needs to be done within the school environment to identify children who are displaying certain learning-specific traits so that again they can access the support needed to overcome their difficulties and flourish within the school environment.

Children with SEN may be extremely gifted, irrespective of their learning disposition. These children must be empowered and mobilised with strategies and techniques that will reverse the downward spiral of their educational experience into an upward spiral of success by building a healthy self-esteem and confidence, along with the skills needed to be successful. This requires an understanding of their specific learning flow. For example, if a child is diagnosed with ADHD, educators should make their learning experience a more creative one, so that the child is able to learn and make good progress.

Gifted and talented children

Perhaps surprisingly, children who are categorised as 'gifted and talented' are also at risk of becoming NEET. This is because they are not sufficiently stimulated to avoid boredom within the school environment. In some cases, this may cause these children to lose motivation and/or misbehave, which can lead to underachievement at GCSE level and, consequently, the prospect of becoming NEET.

Parental involvement

Parental involvement is key to preventing children from becoming NEET. Navigating the educational maze is, at best, challenging, but parents and educators need to be aware of the options available and know what to do at each educational milestone to maximise a child's attainment. This will be the subject of the next chapter.

It is also essential for parents to adopt an appropriate parenting model, as some styles have been shown to make children more susceptible to becoming NEET and low levels of parental support are known to lead to underachievement in children.[44] Different parenting models and their impacts will be discussed in more detail in Chapter 6.

The key thing to appreciate is that where you are now does not have to determine your child's destination. Regardless of what has happened to us in the past, we are empowered to handle future events by adopting an empowering mindset and effective learning strategy with support. This is something we will discuss further later in the book.

Summary

Instead of unlocking their potential and finding their greatness, some children unfortunately become NEET, which has negative impacts on both their life and wider society. Certain – often inter-related – factors make a child more vulnerable to this outcome, but no child is destined to become NEET and these factors can be mitigated when you have the right knowledge, understanding and effort to align educational strategy with learning flow. There are several ways that parents, educators and policymakers can contribute to reducing the likelihood of children becoming NEET, not least working to improve school attendance so that every single child, irrespective of their learning disposition, has access to good education and can enjoy academic achievement and success. In the following chapters, we will see how this can be achieved.

PART TWO

UNLOCKING YOUR CHILD'S POTENTIAL

Part Two will outline the method I have developed for unlocking children's potential. The Inspire Your Greatness Method is founded on seven principles – the 7Ps. Once the principles are put into practice and internalised, your child will be empowered to achieve their greatness. Principle one is Picture: having a clear picture of what it is you want to achieve, because seeing is the basis of all achievement. Then comes Parent – that's you – because the household environment has been proven to be a make-or-break factor in children's success in life. Next is Programme, a blueprint that will put your child in a position to enjoy a life and career on their terms, that will enable them to develop the habits and behaviours necessary to achieve and sustain success, that will literally programme them for success. Our next P, Partnership, is all about working together with other professional agencies to put that programme into action, to inspire greatness and unlock your child's potential. Of course, like any new pattern of learning or development, this requires Practice. As we have learned, for a child to have a successful career and a fulfilled life, they must follow their Passion, the sixth P. Once these first six principles are in place, you will have set your child on the Path to achieving greatness.

5

Picture

Part One emphasised the importance of believing in your child's greatness. With this belief, you will be able to see their potential and know that unlocking it is possible. It is commonly said that 'seeing is believing', but in the case of your child's success, believing is seeing. The picture that is firmly planted in your mind's eye will determine what can be achieved, so this picture should be empowering. Whatever you believe is possible can become your reality. Believing determines what you see and what you experience in your life – and your child's life.

As parents, you set the scene for your child. In their early years, your child will only believe what you have instilled in them, what you have shown them is attainable. You set the standard. This means that not only must you be committed to supporting your child in finding their greatness, but you must also walk on a journey to uncover *your* greatness. You must have the conviction to pursue your passion, without apology.

A perfect example is Creola Katherine Johnson, an American mathematician who worked for NASA in the 1960s. She worked tirelessly on calculations of orbital mechanics in the belief that it was possible for a spacecraft to land on the moon. She could see this happening in her mind and, on 20 July 1969, Neil Armstrong became the first man to set foot on the moon. His success can be attributed to her picture and belief that what she could see with her mind's eye was possible.

Another example is Henry Ford, who dreamed that one day he would be able to produce cars at affordable prices for ordinary people. As a result of his belief, the impossible became possible – mass production, as he had imagined it, became a reality. Could he have believed that the Ford Motor Company would today produce more than a million cars a year? Quite likely.

A third example is Bill Gates, who saw with his mind's eye that one day there would be a personal computer in every household. Most households now have computers. Not only that, but these days we even have computers in our pockets.

These three examples have one thing in common: the impossible became possible. The believer saw the vision as a possibility, not an impossibility. They dared to believe, just as you must, as your child must. When you believe, the impossible can become your reality.

Fulfilment

Have you ever read or heard about a person who appears to be successful externally, who has all the accolades, the cars, the houses, the prestigious lifestyle, the connections, the money, achievement upon achievement – yet they still feel empty? As humans, we can achieve more than we might believe possible, but is it worth it if we feel unfulfilled in our endeavours? We can gain the whole world but lose our soul.

As we discussed at the beginning of the book, I encourage you to redefine your notion of success. This requires a belief that you were born with a purpose. You were fashioned with gifts and talents that are unique to you. These are the ingredients of your passion and your purpose. Again, it is all about living inside-out rather than – like those collecting accolades and success symbols – outside-in. Make no mistake, living inside-out means you can have all those things and still be fulfilled in what you are doing. This is a lesson you must learn so that you can model self-belief and purposeful living for your child.

True success is defined by the legacy you leave. The reason for your existence is not about you, but about the people's lives that will one day be transformed as a direct result of your gifts and talents. It is essential that you dream about your ideal life, that you see it and believe in it with all your heart, because in doing so you will find new possibilities and opportunities open up before you – things that were once impossible.

The first step towards living inside-out and finding fulfilment is to be absolutely clear on your answer to the ultimate question: 'What is the reason for my existence?' What is the one thing that you were put on this earth to do? This is your purpose. When you are clear on your purpose, you become intentional about your daily pursuits. Every decision you make will be aligned to your purpose. You may have heard it said that it's not good to be a busy fool – a busy fool does many things, but none of them is linked to a clear purpose.

The next thing to realise is that your purpose must always be linked to service. It is your ability to serve with excellence and with passion that will determine your wealth. In a business context, how you reach your target audience is based on identifying, what do they need right now and how can you meet that need? Not only that, how can you make them *feel*?

The acid test of whether you are living a life of purpose at work is to look at your diary or review your last month's events and ask yourself: 'When I was completing these activities, was I excited? Was I full of happy anticipation? Or, did I feel drained, fed up? Was I waiting for it to be over?' If your answers were yes,

yes, no and no, congratulations – you have a passion-driven career. If they were the reverse, it could be time to review your career and make a change.

Finding a passion-driven career starts with asking how you can best serve the world. The answer is always through your unique gifts and talents. In doing so, rest assured, not only will you be fulfilled in your career, your relationships and your life, but your children will also be fulfilled in theirs. You will be cocreating and raising a generation that is not only fulfilled at work but will also enjoy more fulfilling relationships and contribute value to society. They in turn will then raise their children to do the same. In having a passion-driven career yourself, you will be inspiring and supporting the child(ren) in your care to pursue and achieve a passion-driven career for themselves.

You cannot give what you do not have. Imagine a cup, which you fill with water until it is overflowing. As part of your self-care strategy, you must fill yourself first, meet your own spiritual, emotional, physical, intellectual and social needs. Then, when your cup runs over, from the overflow you can empower the child(ren) in your care to fulfil their potential and find a passion-driven career. You cannot live in the shadow of someone else's vision. You must have your own vision for *your* life, based on *your* purpose.

Personal leadership versus management

Success requires leadership, but leadership requires a clear vision for your life and clear goals. Unless you have these for yourself, you will be unable to empower your child to discover their own gifts and talents and fulfil their purpose. If you do not have a clear vision and goals, it is likely that you are living within an occupational rather than a vocational paradigm (these are discussed in more detail in Chapter 11), one that is linked only to personal management.

A true leader of people is first a leader of their own life, and personal leadership is about being clear on your purpose – the 'why' of your existence. The vision for your life is your purpose in picture form, so again requires you to be completely clear on your purpose. True personal leadership is governed by your purpose, whereas personal management is about considering what resources are needed to make your personal vision a reality.

Personal leadership asks the 'what' and 'why' questions, while the personal management paradigm asks 'how' questions. For example, personal leadership would involve asking, 'What is my life purpose?' while someone engaged in personal management would ask, 'How can I achieve my purpose?'

There is a misconception that pursuing your purpose does not put food on the table. As we have learned, money follows service.

Personal management is about the resources that are needed to ensure that your personal vision becomes a reality. As you can see, both paradigms are important, but personal leadership comes first and personal management comes second. Nothing 'just happens' or happens by chance. True success comes from awareness and effective execution of purpose-driven vision-based success principles.

Summary

Seeing is believing. This chapter has talked about the power of belief and what you can see for yourself, and for your child, in your mind's eye. What you see and believe in will determine what life holds for you – this is as true for you as it is for your child. In picturing your vision for your future, you may need to redefine what you consider success to be. Your focus should always be on finding fulfilment, leaving a legacy and following your purpose. This will involve both personal leadership and personal management and is the approach to life you should be modelling for your child.

What is your dream? What vision have you had since you were a child? What dream does your child have? What are they hoping to be, to achieve? If you can picture the answers to these questions, you are well on your way to realising those dreams. Dare to believe in what you see.

6

Parent

A child's home environment, meaning their family background, consists of all the family and material resources present within the home that affect the child's life, such as the parent's level of education, occupation, socioeconomic status and the socialising facilities available in the house.[45] Beyond that, home should be an enjoyable, happy place where we live, laugh and learn.[46] Children need stable, supportive home environments to enhance their cognitive, emotional and physical wellbeing.[47] It has been shown that parents who provide a warm and responsive home environment and who encourage exploration accelerate their children's intellectual development.

A child's home environment impacts their academic performance. This means that, as a parent, you can influence your child's academic achievement by shaping their behaviours and attitudes towards school.[48]

Positive attitudes towards education and school have been shown to be associated with increased academic performance in children.[49]

Connection

The Unlocking Potential framework will help you connect with your child by learning their communication preferences. Every child perceives love in a unique way, and prefers to receive it in a particular way – through praise, a prize or participation. This is their Unlocking Potential Communication Preference.

Praise

Praise means affirming your child's good qualities, gifts and talents. There are different ways of giving praise, and some may be more valuable than others. Ability praise is a common way to provide feedback on good performance that can boost children's sense of efficacy and motivate their learning.[50] Effort praise leads children to focus on the process of work and the development of learning skills, leading to greater persistence and good performance after setbacks. Effort praise tends to put children into an empowering mindset; it conveys the message, 'You can develop these skills because you're working hard.' This kind of praise given to one- to three-year-olds has been shown to predict their motivational framework five years later,[51] and children's self-evaluation is positively impacted when hearing even a small amount of effort praise.[52] Praise for intelligence, on the other hand, can undermine children's motivation and performance.[53]

Prize

An alternative to giving your child praise, one which has similar benefits, is to give them a prize. You must make sure, however, that the prize is aligned with their gifts, talents and interests.

Participation

To make a connection with your child, it is essential to give them your undivided attention through conversation or joint activities, as well as plenty of physical contact (for instance, hugs).

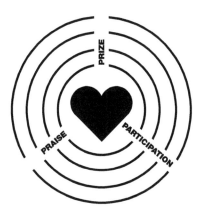

Three keys to connection

Cultivation

As well as connection, unlocking potential requires cultivation. Cultivation is the promotion of positive character traits, which are the outcome of discipline. I define cultivation as the development of character excellence using a moral compass to ensure that a code of behaviour is adhered to. The purpose of cultivation is to empower your child to develop qualities they currently lack, a lack that will always manifest in behaviour.

Over time, effective cultivation will empower your child to make ethical decisions; it will foster their emotional intelligence, by helping them to not only become aware of their emotions but also to connect with and channel them in the right way; and it will promote self-discipline – one of the key ingredients of academic success.

For cultivation to be empowering and transformational, three things must be considered and adopted:

- **Parent–child relationship.** The parent–child relationship is the bedrock of cultivation. For cultivation to be effective, this bond must be strong. Researchers have reported that parent–child interactions, specifically stimulating and responsive parenting practices, are important influences on a child's academic development.[54]

- **Positive behaviour strategies.** A child's behaviour is a mirror image of their psychological state. Positive reinforcement is a great tool to encourage the behaviour you want to cultivate. Through positive reinforcement, you can cultivate a desirable character, help your child develop their gifts and talents and clearly communicate your expectations to them.

- **Strategies for discouraging unwanted behaviours.** Consequences are great tools to help your children learn from their mistakes so that they're empowered to make better choices in the future. When giving your child consequences, you should:

  - Make sure they're appropriate for their age, temperament and misbehaviour.

  - Communicate your expectations in advance, so your child is clear about why they are receiving a consequence.

  - Always treat your child with dignity and respect.

Three cornerstones of empowering cultivation

Parenting principles

Good parenting is founded on six principles. When applied properly and consistently, these principles will help you unlock your child's potential.

1. Language

Patience is the ability to proactively wait for your child to come around to an idea or request. It involves communicating to your child what you expect from them without becoming irritated. It also enables you to speak the truth to your child in an empowering way. Words are the expression of your thoughts, which can be either disempowering (limiting thoughts) or empowering. What thoughts are you speaking to your child? Do the words you speak build emotional resilience, confidence, healthy self-esteem and a 'can-do' attitude? Or do they leave your child emotionally depleted, and lower their confidence and self-esteem?

In the heat of the moment, patience will enable you to speak empowering words to your child, giving them a sense of emotional security, belonging and hope.

2. Kindness

Kindness means serving your child by sincerely volunteering your gifts, talents, time and resources. Kindness is a state of being, one which always asks, 'How can I best serve my child? How can my gifts, talents, time and resources be used to unlock my child's potential?'

3. Humility

Humility is being able to recognise your own values, and those of others, while acknowledging the need for guidance in your developmental areas. Humility is a quality that enables you to accept correction. Our age does not necessarily mean we know it all. We and our children are interdependent, learning from each other; together we can achieve more.

4. Forgiveness

Forgiveness is an intentional decision to release any anger and resentment felt towards someone who has hurt you. It's often said that 'it takes a village to raise a child'. If your relationships with people in your support network are strained because forgiveness is needed and hasn't been given, this will negatively affect the wellbeing of your child, directly or indirectly.

Forgiveness is a great strategy for guarding your mind. Your mind is the seat from which either positive or negative emotions will find expression in your life. In fact, science has shown lack of forgiveness to be a potential cause of increased heart disease[55] and increase the onset of mental health challenges and stress.[56]

Since children are like sponges, soaking up the influences of their environment, the emotions we carry with us will be picked up by our children. Our emotional wellbeing, as parents, can therefore either disempower or empower our children. I encourage you, today, if there is someone you have not forgiven, to seek out the necessary support to begin the process of forgiveness. You will feel better for it, and so will your child.

5. Courtesy

Put simply, courtesy is politeness. Parents' behaviour behind closed doors will influence a child's behaviour in public, so it is vital to model courteous behaviour at home. Do you demand that your child obey your requests? Or do you ask them politely? You cannot expect your children to show courtesy to you and to others if you have not modelled courteous behaviour toward and in front of your children.

6. Modelling

Your parenting psychology shapes your behaviour as a parent. If you don't like your child's behaviour, you need to look at the behaviour you're modelling, as children will mirror what they observe in their household environment.

Before reading on, ask yourself these questions:

- How can I demonstrate patience to my child?

- How can I serve my child to unlock their potential?

- How can I demonstrate humility when interacting with my child?

- Who can I forgive today?

- When did I last demonstrate courteous behaviour in front of my child?

- Am I behaving the way I want my child to behave?

Not all parents apply these principles consistently or in the same way, and different approaches to and emphasis on these key areas result in different parenting models, which differ in their capacity to unlock potential in a child. I broadly categorise parenting into three models, based on how they prioritise connection and cultivation, which we will discuss in turn.

Free-for-all parenting

As parents, how effective we are in unlocking potential in our children depends on the parenting 'model' we adopt. A commonly used model is what I call 'free-for-all parenting'. As shown in the diagram below, the

free-for-all parent heavily relies on connection and
limits cultivation.

Free-for-all parenting model

Some indicators of a free-for-all parenting style can be
found in households where:

- There are no or limited rules for the child – the
  parent frequently uses bribery (eg food, toys or
  gifts) to encourage the behaviour they're seeking
  in their child.

- The child lacks self-discipline due to a lack of
  routine.

- The parent sees themselves as a friend to their
  child rather than a parent (eg they ask their child
  to make decisions that aren't age-appropriate).

Consequences of free-for-all parenting

- **Underachievement.** Children of free-for-all
  parents tend to underachieve compared with
  their peers. This is largely due to their parents'
  lack of expectations for them.

- **Poor time-management skills.** Free-for-all
  parents seldom embed family routines.

Without routines, children do not learn to regulate themselves. This results in poor time-management skills.

- **Poor decisions.** Free-for-all parents tend not to instil a moral compass in their children by way of cultivation, so their children may struggle to make the right decisions.

- **Delinquency.** Children raised by free-for-all parents have a higher risk of delinquent behaviour, due to lack of cultivation.[57]

- **Low emotional intelligence.** In the free-for-all parenting model, children are not encouraged to develop the capacity to manage their emotions. This means that in adulthood they are likely to struggle when faced with stressful situations.

Disempowering parenting

When adopting the disempowering parenting model, which is somewhat of a reversal of the 'free-for-all' model, parents focus on cultivation with little regard for connection. This again creates an imbalance, as shown in the diagram below.

Disempowering parenting model

Some features of a disempowering parenting style include:

- Punishment being used as a form of cultivation, with a focus on 'what' rather than 'why'. Parents who use this model tend to tell their children what they have done wrong but never discuss why that behaviour is wrong. The results of the punishment are largely driven by fear and are short-lived.

- Parents who use the disempowering parenting model often encourage their children to pursue careers that will give them social and economic status ('keeping up with the Joneses'), rather than to pursue and unlock their natural talents and gifts.

- Disempowering parents tend to believe that children should be seen and not heard. They seldom give their children the opportunity to develop independence by empowering them to make age-appropriate decisions.

- Disempowering parents do not prioritise emotional connection with their children. They rarely communicate their love for their child through the child's Unlocking Potential Communication Preference; rather, they focus on communicating their own expectations, boundaries and rules.

Consequences of disempowering parenting

- **Low self-esteem.** A child's self-esteem is built over time through their interactions with their parents as well as life situations. Parents who adopt the disempowering parenting model are likely to raise children with low self-esteem.

- **Lack of confidence.** The children of disempowering parents tend to lack confidence because they have not been allowed to make decisions and meet self-imposed aims.

- **Negativity.** Disempowered children tend to have a negative outlook on life. They focus on their weaknesses rather than their strengths, and on what could go wrong in a given situation.

- **Approval-seeking.** Children who are raised according to the disempowering parenting model seek to earn their parents' approval through obedience and successes, as they do not feel that their parents' love is unconditional. Surprisingly, though, they also find it difficult to accept recognition from others.

- **Anger.** Children of disempowering parents are likely to be more aggressive, due to the frustration that results from their feeling a lack of connection.

Empowering parenting

To empower someone means 'To give them the means to achieve something, for example to become stronger or more successful.'[58] Empowering parents enable their children to flourish in their transition into adulthood. They take a balanced approach to pursuing connection and cultivation. They understand that to effectively cultivate their child, it is first necessary to connect with them; that, with the right balance of efforts, they will build a strong, healthy and tenacious relationship with their child.

CONNECTION   CULTIVATION

Empowering parenting model

Some indicators of empowering parenting include:

- A child of empowering parents will be encouraged to discover their unique blend of gifts and talents for themselves, and to use these to pursue a career that will enable them to serve the world.

- They are likely to have high self-esteem and confidence because their voice is always heard, even if their parents do not agree with what they are saying.

- Consequences are favoured over punishment, as a long-term strategy rather than a short-term measure. Empowering parents seek to understand the root cause of their child's misbehaviour and they will use consequences to bridge the gap between the misbehaviour and the desired behaviour. A child raised by empowering parents will tend to be open to receiving consequences; they are clear about what their parents expect from them.

Benefits of empowering parenting

Children raised according to the empowering parenting model are likely to:

- Have high emotional intelligence, resulting in a higher IQ
- Be good role models for others
- Have high self-esteem
- Be confident
- Have good social skills
- Be happy

Clearly, you want to strive to be an empowering parent, rather than a free-for-all or disempowering parent. Your strategy for achieving this should be based on the six parenting principles outlined in this chapter, which are encapsulated in these four guidelines:

1. **Share your expectations.** Consult with your children and together devise seven Unlocking Potential Rules. The purpose of these rules is to communicate to your children the expectations you have for your household. Including your children in the process will teach them about personal responsibility and accountability.

2. **Pre-determine consequences.** The basis of effective cultivation is consequences, not punishment. Punishment has only short-term benefit (rooted in fear) while consequences, when applied correctly, will teach a child valuable lessons in a supportive, nurturing and respectful way.

3. **Cultivate proactively.** Model the behaviour you wish to see in your child and always reinforce positive behaviour.

4. **Be consistent.** The strategy you adopt will be successful only if you apply it consistently; nothing will undermine its effectiveness more than constantly changing expectations, consequences and modelled behaviour.

Summary

As a parent, you play perhaps the most vital role in setting your child on the path to greatness and unlocking their potential, and your influence over their values, behaviour and vision is vast. Your child's home environment is crucial to both their personal and academic development; within it, you should be focusing on connection and cultivation. To connect most effectively with your child, you should identify their communication preference – whether they respond best to praise, prizes or participation. This will enable you to cultivate good character in your child through a strong parent–child relationship in which you employ positive behaviour strategies and discourage negative behaviours.

You should also look to apply the six parenting principles: language, kindness, humility, forgiveness, courtesy and modelling. In doing so, you should strive to adopt an empowering parenting model by sharing your expectations of your child, establishing consequences for negative behaviour, proactively cultivating positive behaviour and traits, and most importantly, being consistent in your approach.

7

Programme

Have you ever wondered how some people make success look easy? They speak about their goals with vigour and passion, and genuinely believe that what they envision will materialise. When they speak about their vision, they are energised, they get excited, they smile, knowing that it will become a reality. They understand that their vision is simply their purpose in image form. They begin with the end in mind.

Daily endeavours are a reflection, a forecast of what is to come. This means that success (or failure) is predictable. Evaluating your daily activities to ensure they are always aligned to your purpose will increase your productivity and progress. Take stock of your life today. Are you achieving the goals you've set in accordance with your purpose, according to your passion? How are you managing your time to fully realise your vision, your children's vision, your spouse's vision? Are you living in the shadow of someone else's vision for your life? Or are you living in the true substance of your life?

Habits

Habits can be defined as 'learned sequences of acts that have become automatic responses to specific cues and are functional in obtaining certain goals or end states.'[59] Understanding how habits are formed requires some understanding of how the human brain works. The brain is made up of two parts: the conscious and the subconscious minds. The conscious mind is responsible for rational thinking and can act as a filter for what we perceive, establishing what we believe to be true. That information is then passed to the subconscious mind, where it is fleshed out and informs our habits. The basis of forming habits is the repetition of specific behaviours, with the quality of the habits formed being measured in terms of the 'automaticity' and 'efficiency' of those behaviours.[60] In other words, good habits are those that do not require conscious thought but are an involuntary reaction to a cue. The quality of a habit is determined not only by its efficiency, but also by its controllability.[61] Habits take anything from eighteen days to eight months to form; the average appears to be around two months, irrespective of the habit's complexity.[62]

Habits are key to success. The key is to build habits that will enable your success to become automatic, inevitable. Success is automatic if it is built on the right foundations: belief systems, routines and actions that are directed towards your goal and aligned to your purpose. To establish whether your habits are driving automatic success, ask yourself:

- What habits are inherent in your life today?
- Are these habits serving you, or are they preventing you from walking in your greatness?
- What habits do your children have right now? Are these habits empowering or disempowering them?

Success is a form of feedback. Success tells you that you have got the right habits in place, that you are applying the right principles. But what are the 'right' habits? Let's explore this.

Empowering habits

An example of an empowering habit is optimal water intake. According to research, optimal water intake is 1,300–3,300ml per day, depending on gender, age and metabolic factors.[63] Water intake below the optimal level would leave a child or adult dehydrated, the effects of which include poor concentration, lack of alertness and short memory capacity.[64]

Another example of an empowering habit relates to financial management. Research suggests the parents' financial literacy level is causally linked to what they saw, learned and experienced in their childhood[65] and that parental actions and characteristics have a greater impact on a child's financial capability than formal financial education in school.[66] It is, therefore, crucial that parents model good financial habits to children so that they can develop a healthy mindset and attitude toward money and be able to manage their own money effectively. Think about when your child earns or is given money. Are they allowed to spend it all straight away? Or are they encouraged to save/invest some of their money and/or give a portion to charity?

Family routines

Family routines can be defined as repeated behaviours involving a minimum time commitment and tasks that require little conscious thought.[67,68] Empowering family routines give the home environment a predictable structure that creates a stable emotional climate that will support child development and academic success.[69] For family routines to be robust, they require communication, commitment and continuity.[70]

Some strategies for developing empowering family routines are to:

- Keep a diary for one month, making notes of what time you do specific activities – for example, what time you and your child wake up in the mornings, what time you study. This is important to identify time wastage and any disempowering routines.

- Develop daily priorities and activities within a structure that requires less conscious thought.

- Pre-empt hurdles to your daily priorities and activities and plan potential solutions to these in advance.

It is well documented that continuity – or consistency – is key. Routines are vital for children. One routine I would urge you to put in place immediately is a solid bedtime routine, as good sleep habits are the bedrock of an empowered family.[71,72]

Sleep

Sleep is a foundation of academic success: research has shown that sleep deprivation is one of the primary causes of poor school performance, resulting in school grades that are below target.[73] And yet, the same research found that 70% of school-age children do not get the amount of sleep needed to aid child development, leading to academic success. The recommended number of hours sleep, according to the American Academy of Pediatrics, are:[74]

- Infants under 1 year: 12–16 hours

- Children 1–2 years old: 11–14 hours

- Children 3–5 years old: 10–13 hours

- Children 6–12 years old: 9–12 hours

- Teenagers 13–18 years old: 8–10 hours

One of the major causes of sleep deprivation today is the use of electronic devices late in the evening.[75] A big contributor to this is gaming devices; in particular, research has shown that violent video games put a child's body in a stressful state, causing a fight-or-flight response, which increases both blood pressure and heart rate.[76]

Some signs that your child is *not* getting adequate sleep are when:

- They do not fall asleep within fifteen to thirty minutes of going to bed – this is because they are overtired.

- They are unable to wake up independently at their routine getting up time without constant nagging.

- They are unable to perform through the day without the need to nap.[77]

If sleep deprivation is prolonged, it can not only lead to underachievement in the school environment,[78] but also cause health issues, such as:

- Increase in unhealthy snacking, leading to greater consumption of carbohydrates;[79] this will cause poor concentration and memory,[80] negatively influencing learning.[81]

- Increased risk of accidents, mental health challenges, obesity and diabetes.[82]

- General lack of physical and emotional wellbeing that could hamper development.[83,84]

- Impatience, mood swings, hyperactivity – sometimes masking traits of ADHD[85] – and even aggressive behaviour.[86]

If your child displays any of the above signs or behaviours, it is time to make swift changes to your child's routine to ensure that they get the recommended amount of sleep. If in doubt, seek assistance.

Remember that sleep deprivation can also affect you. Adults should aim for a minimum of seven hours per night in order to maintain good health.[87] The health risks to adults of not getting the recommended amount of sleep include obesity, diabetes, heart disease, depression, weight gain, impaired immune function, increased errors, greater risks of accidents and hypertension.[88] In addition to the avoidance of these negative effects, one of the noted health benefits of getting adequate sleep is a low risk of infection, as sleep is known to strengthen the immune system.[89]

Summary

Working with children, young people and adults for several years in a variety of environments, I have come to understand that daily practices are a forecast of what is to come, so reviewing these is essential. For example, your child may have said to you, 'I want to achieve a Grade 8' (formerly A*), but if their daily practice does not reflect a Grade 8, how will they achieve this? If you, as a parent, want the child in your care to excel academically, to grow into a vibrant person and to one day stand out and make a difference, small changes are needed today. These small changes will enable your child to unlock their potential and walk in their greatness.

8

Partnership

Partnership

At the heart of every successful enterprise is collaboration and teamwork, just as in sport. And all sports have necessary rules by which the players abide. Every member of the team has a specific role, and the players work together to achieve the desired result: winning the game. If the players do not work together, the consequences would be disastrous – organised chaos, discord, lack of leadership, conflicting aims and strategies... The team would perform below their potential and would likely lose the game.

The same principle applies to you as a parent, educator, or policymaker, whether you have a child in your immediate care within your household, or whether you influence children's development more widely through education. Their ability to walk in their greatness is determined by your ability to work in partnership with others. An effective partnership is a team sport – it begins with the end in mind, with an understanding of what results you are looking to obtain and how each team member will contribute to achieving this.

Benefits of partnership

Research has clearly identified that increased parental collaboration between parents and school not only improves children's academic performance,[90] but also positively influences their cognitive development and socialisation.[91] This is evidenced in the positive behaviour of students, increased intrinsic motivation and improved relationships between teachers and students and between students and other students.[92] Moreover, being the focus of a positive partnership improves a child's self-concept and instils a belief that they have skills necessary to succeed academically.[93]

You will be doing your child a grave disservice if you simply drop them off at school and leave them to figure out for themselves how to learn most effectively. Unity is strength. Unity is key. All teamwork relies on clearly defined outcomes. The outcome you are looking to achieve, working in partnership with your child's school and any other involved parties, is the basis for the unlocking of your child's greatness; your efforts should be focused entirely on that outcome. Like all teamwork, this partnership must be built on sound communication and mutual respect.

Fulfilled and successful children require a good education – in the true sense of the word – and good education does not happen by chance. It is the product of an effective teaching and learning process, coupled with the effort of the teacher, the school, the students, parents and their home environment. There must be a connection between these elements; they must work together. The most effective way to achieve this is through the Triad Partnership Model. It is so named because it is built on three legs, like a stool. The three legs give it balance, ensuring it never wobbles.

Triad Partnership Model

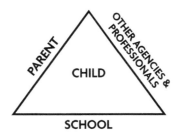

Triad Partnership Model

Effective partnership is based on a collaborative and cooperative relationship between the school, the parent and any relevant agencies/professionals to unlock your child's potential.[94] It is essential that all partners work together as a team to ignite the intrinsic motivation in your child – the driver of both academic success and your child's general development.[95]

Forming a strong partnership with respectful and resourceful communication between all parties is key to raising children who are happy, fulfilled and transformed, who go on to have a passion-driven career and enjoy the success they deserve.

It is therefore essential that parents are strategic in choosing the right schools and professionals to be part of your Triad Partnership, so that your child is inspired, motivated and empowered to achieve greatness. Let's now look at each of the three elements of the triad in turn.

Parents

As we learned in Chapter 6, the first key to unlocking your child's potential so that they can walk in their greatness, is the parent(s). Ultimately, as a parent, you are your child's primary educator. Research has demonstrated that when there is low parental involvement in a child's educational development,[96] this has a significant impact on their grades, which can make or break their academic progress. It is therefore essential for you, as a parent, to work in partnership with your child's school – as their secondary educator – to ensure that you pass on vital information that will support the school in unlocking your child's potential.

It is easy to point fingers and blame others for your child not reaching their full potential. But all success begins with us as parents taking responsibility for our actions and/or inactions. One such action is how you choose to engage (or not) with your child's school, which will largely determine the success or failure of their school career.

The type of parent you are will influence how you partner with your child's school and the results that can be achieved through this partnership. It has been suggested that there are three types of parents:

Passive parents

Passive parents are not aware of the school curriculum or their child's progress. They seldom attend parents' evenings and do not fully support their children with their schoolwork. Since the school staff may see these parents only a few times a year, they often do not know who they are. Not surprisingly, the children of passive parents are likely to underachieve.

These parents assign the role of primary educator to their child's teachers. They do not take full responsibility for their child's progress. In some cases, this may not be through choice, but due to lacking the relevant knowledge, skills and confidence to collaborate with outside professionals/institutions/agencies to compensate for their knowledge and skill deficit. This type of parent's communication style tends to be more reactive than proactive; for example, they might have contact with the school only when an incident has occurred.

Present parents

These parents will attend events intended to support their child's progress and will assist with their child's homework, but they will not extend their involvement to strategic roles within the school that would accelerate their child's progress further. They are participants in the school environment, but their participation is limited.

Partner parents

Partner parents see their role as working with their child's school, as well as other agencies and professionals, to help their child develop. They ensure that their child's school attendance is at least 95% (see Chapter 2) and adopt a proactive approach to supporting their child's teachers, who they know will have a positive influence on their child's academic development. They are constantly asking, 'How can I collaborate to improve outcomes for the school that will positive impact my child?' They attend all parents' evenings and are fully engaged in the school's wider activities. They strategically engage in other agency or professional services to break their children's glass ceiling and/or support with strategic decisions that will improve their children's holistic development. They take a role in the parent–teacher association (PTA) and may become school governors to ensure that they have a voice in the school's strategic decision-making.

If you have identified yourself as a passive or present parent, I urge you to take steps to address this and work to proactively and respectfully partner with your child's school. Being a partner parent is essential for your child's progress. As discussed in Chapter 6, parenting should follow an inside-out approach with an empowering attitude towards education that will accelerate your child's academic progress.[97] Moreover, your attitude towards education in the home environment will shape your child's classroom behaviour, either positively or negatively influencing their teacher–student relationship.[98]

School

Your child's relationship with their schoolteachers is an indicator of their likely academic achievement. For a teacher to inspire your child to realise their greatness, a positive relationship is imperative. The teacher must see them as an individual and be able to clearly identify their strengths as well as the development areas where they can unlock their potential. A positive teacher–student relationship is characterised by a lack of dependency and conflict.[99] This kind of relationship is impossible to maintain and develop if conflict between teacher and student arises due to the child's misbehaviour or the teacher's skillset with supporting children, ie children who have special educational needs and are not supported through their learning flow are likely to misbehave. If the teacher is not armed with the knowledge to support these children, their misbehaviour can be the mask for undiagnosed learning needs. It takes a teacher/practitioner of compassion, discernment and knowledge to look beyond the misbehaviour manifesting and see the child's potential while providing the necessary support to bridge this gap. Teacher–parent collaboration is essential to determine the root cause of any such misbehaviour and resolve the conflict. If you are to partner with your child's school effectively, there must be two-way and respectful communication and exchange of information for the betterment of your child. This can only be achieved by partner parents.

Other agencies and professionals

The third 'leg' of the Triad Partnership is other relevant agencies and professionals. This would include any private tutors, medical professionals, counsellors, therapists or specialists working with your child on a specific challenge or condition. Or it might be a learning coach, someone who has an empowering relationship with their students, seeing their life vision as clearly as possible and supporting them to unlock their potential. They will also help parents to develop a strategic plan to bring this vision to fruition through improved academic performance.

A learning coach will help your child to identify their glass ceiling (their disempowering thoughts) and inspire them to break through it. They will make your child aware of habitual behaviours that are holding them back from achieving their full potential. And they will support you, as parents, in navigating the educational maze and working with the school to support your child's academic success.

The benefits of working with a learning coach include:

- Improved school behaviour

- Better time management, particularly around revision

- Greater self-awareness and an improved self-concept

- Confidence to break through barriers and achieve success

- Improved academic performance by way of grades

Summary

To unlock your child's potential so that they can walk in their greatness, it is essential that you be a partner parent and engage in a three-way partnership with your child's school and other appropriate agencies and professionals. It is only by working as a team that you will empower your child to achieve their full potential. To contribute meaningfully to this collaboration, you should strive to be a 'partner parent', rather than a passive or present parent. Being the focus of the combined efforts of an empowering team will strengthen your child's self-concept and self-belief and ignite their intrinsic motivation.

9

Practice

Are you able to think of a time when you learned a new skill and were able to demonstrate complete mastery within five minutes? It's likely that the answer will be a resounding NO. Now think about when (if) you learned to drive. Can you recall the overwhelming feeling of hopelessness as you tried to control the accelerator, gear lever and steering wheel, while keeping your eye on the road? Most likely, that's a resounding YES. How did you progress from that feeling of hopelessness to the mastery of driving – the point where it required no conscious thought? The answer is, of course, through PRACTICE.

You will have heard it said that practice makes perfect, but this is inaccurate. Practice makes *permanent*. What is the difference? This relates to how the brain learns, something we will explore in this chapter.

Neurons are the building blocks of the brain, with more than 86 billion of them.[100] Learning takes place when neurons in the brain respond to a stimulus in the environment by making new neuronal connections, which alter the structure of the brain. This capacity of the brain to re-structure itself is known as neuroplasticity and allows us to learn at any age in life: you are never too old to learn.[101] In fact, learning a new skill is proven to slow cognitive ageing, helping to keep neurodegenerative diseases such as Alzheimer's at bay.[102]

The strength of the neuronal connection (synapse) determines the effectiveness of the information processing and storage in the long-term memory.[103] The stronger the neuronal connection, the greater the recall of information at will – in other words, the better your memory. A strong neuronal connection is dependent on the repetition of the learning material through deliberate practice; lack of practice will weaken the neuronal connection – hence the adage, 'Use it or lose it.'

Deliberate practice is 'the engagement in activities designed to raise performance in a specific area' and requires a high degree of concentration; mastery of performance in a given area is reflective of the time dedicated to deliberate practice rather than of innate ability or talent.[104,105] Success in any field, and particularly academia, is dependent on deliberate practice of specific techniques. The knowledge and application of these techniques, formed into habits, will make a young person's academic success automatic – their thinking processes will become clearer, enabling them to make informed decisions based on accurate information.

The thinking process itself comprises a set of electrical signals running through the brain; these are called 'brain waves'. There are five types of brain wave, from low to high frequency (expressed in Hertz (Hz) or cycles per second):

1. Delta waves (0.5–4Hz). These brain waves occur during deep sleep.

2. Theta waves (4–8Hz). These waves occur during deep relaxation and/or light sleep.

3. Alpha waves (8–12Hz). These occur when you are awake but relaxed.

4. Beta waves (12–30Hz). These occur when you are conscious and aware.

5. Gamma waves (30–100Hz). Gamma waves help the brain to process information from different areas.[106]

The significance of the different kinds of brain waves is particularly evident in relation to learning flow.

Learning flow

Imagine a warm, sunny day with a clear blue sky. You are sitting by a canal. The canal is full of water that is flowing smoothly, seemingly at its own pace. In fact, the flow is determined by the frequency with which the lock gates on the canal are opened and closed, as each time this happens a certain volume of water is moved downstream. What is most important to the canal is that fresh water is flowing through it, to maintain its vitality. Without this, it would stagnate.

We can relate this image to learning flow. As with a canal, when the lock gates are open, the learning can flow through seamlessly. However, if the gates remain closed, or only ajar, the flow slows down or stops altogether. Those gates represent the barriers that slow learning down and it is imperative that you help your child to understand the learning flow and how to keep the gates open.

There are two types of learning flow, two types of learner: academic and creative learner. Is your child an academic learner or a creative learner? It is essential to know this, because each type of learner should apply a different learning strategy – it can be harmful to adopt a strategy that is not aligned to your child's learning type. It is rather like trying to put a square peg in a round hole, or like asking a fish to breathe air and walk. You should have a clear plan for organising your child's homework and revision, and this will require knowledge of what type of learner they are.

The key thing for parents and/or educators to understand is that identifying and empowering children to enter and remain in their learning flow is necessary for them to reach their full potential.

ANDRE

Andre (not his real name) joined our programme in Year 6. He had a natural flair for English, reading and writing, but maths was his learning barrier – a lock gate closed firmly shut, preventing his learning flow. Whenever he was faced with challenging questions in maths, he became frustrated and unable to provide a satisfactory answer. Through supportive and small group sessions, as well as extra tuition, he was able to build his confidence to push open the lock gate and develop a can-do approach. Within six months, he had moved into the top set in maths.

Learning systems

Having worked with children in a variety of learning environments, ranging from mainstream education and tuition centres to Pupil Referral Units (PRUs) and special needs schools, I have learned that academic success is the result of a robust learning system.

What is a learning system? We know that learning is the ability to process information to acquire new knowledge and/or skill, and a system is generally considered a set of methods that combine to achieve a desired outcome. Combining the two concepts, a learning system is the application of a specific set of learning methods to process information. These methods can empower your child to achieve the grades they aspire to and are capable of.

Experience has shown me that whenever a child is underachieving, there is a system malfunction. The job of parents and/or educators is to identify the 'broken' learning system and replace it with a more effective one to help build intrinsic motivation to succeed. How can we identify when a learning system is broken? Three pillars underpin an effective learning system:

Pillar One: Positive state of mind

For a child to learn effectively, the learning system must promote a positive state of mind. If a child is stressed or believes that they cannot achieve something, guess what? They won't. Conversely, if a child believes that they can achieve, they will. We'll talk about this more later in the book. When you are relaxed and free from anxiety, learning is effortless and seamless; you are in your learning flow.

For children and young people to learn, they must be in a relaxed and calm state of mind. To achieve this, their brains must be enabled to use alpha waves as much as possible (see above), which foster creative thoughts and ideas.

Pillar Two: Learning journal

Encourage your child to keep a diary or journal of the events that occur along their learning journey, the successes and the areas requiring development, noting their thoughts, feelings and actions surrounding these events. A learning journal is an amazing tool for unpicking the causes and effects of these events and for bringing clarity around the learning system in place and how it is affecting your child's academic performance.

The specific benefits of keeping a learning journal include the following.

- **Higher grades:** Keeping a learning journal promotes reflective thinking, which identifies the thoughts and actions that contributed to successes, as well as the practices that could or have adversely impacted academic performance.[107]

- **Better working memory:** Writing down negative thoughts and feelings not only significantly improves concentration[108,109] but also frees up the working memory for positive thoughts and feelings.

- **Improved behaviour:** Keeping a learning journal will enable your child to focus on meeting their needs; since human behaviour is a reflection of

met or unmet needs, this will promote better
behaviours.[110]

- **Critical thinking:** Keeping a learning journal
  will help your child to become a critical thinker
  and reflect on their learning.

- **Greater emotional wellbeing:** Keeping a
  learning journal is also therapeutic, as it will
  encourage your child to write down and reflect
  on their innermost thoughts.

- **Stronger immune system:** Since negative
  thoughts and emotions are known to lower the
  immune system response, making a person
  susceptible to illness and disease, keeping a
  journal in which you 'park' negative thoughts
  and emotions can strengthen your immune
  system.[111]

In sum, keeping a learning journal will help your
child − and therefore you − to identify any problems
in their learning system and develop a system that will
more effectively support their academic success. It is
our responsibility as parents and educators to guide
children and young people away from the unwanted
behaviour associated with anxiety and stress and to
explore strategies that will empower them to meet
their unmet needs.

Pillar Three: Memorisation

As we know, learning is the acquisition of knowledge and skills resulting in behavioural change, evidenced in changes to understanding, values and capability.[112] The acquisition of knowledge and skills is the first step of learning, but this information must then be retained in the long-term memory.

Humans have two types of memory: the working memory and the long-term memory. The working memory stores information for only a short period; an example of the working memory in action is remembering a phone number for long enough to write it down. The working memory is able to retrieve information from the long-term memory in order to process that information; and it is this processing function that enables a person to learn. Repetition of information causes neural connections to be formed creating the long-term memory and enabling the processing mechanism without which no effective learning has taken place.[113] True learning requires information to be available for recall a week, a month, twelve months later. This is essential for critical thinking and the ability to synthesise information rather than merely regurgitate it.

One of the most common mistakes made by students is to 'cram' for assessments and exams at the last minute (discussed in more detail later in the book). In doing so, they are relying on their short-term memory to achieve success. Not only is this highly ineffective, but cramming is also a major cause of examination anxiety. Instead, students should carry out a spaced review of knowledge, revising what has been taught periodically and regularly – for example, the day after teaching and then seven, fourteen, twenty-one and twenty-eight days thereafter. Repeated reviews will enable your child to identify gaps in their knowledge and find ways to fill those gaps; this will increase their confidence in those areas and eliminate the need to cram when exams are approaching.

Your child should not depend only on what they have been taught in the classroom, but deepen their knowledge through further independent study. You can help them with this, but it is also a good idea for them to join a study group, where several students review their learning together. This will have benefits beyond their academic learning, in terms of practising teamwork skills and collaborating with others.

Summary

Learning, clearly key to academic success, requires practice if it is to be sustained and knowledge retained in the long term. For effective learning to take place, your child needs to enter their 'learning flow' and apply an effective learning system that is aligned with the type of learner they are. There are three pillars of a good learning system: a positive state of mind, a learning journal and memorisation.

Memorisation requires deliberate and regular practice. In my work, I have come across students with aspirations to achieve a particular grade but no plan in place to take them there, other than last-minute cramming. Get organised so that your child can achieve the success they desire without a struggle. Draw up a study plan, with routine spaced reviews of knowledge, remembering to make room for downtime, for recreational activities, for family and friends. This will optimise your child's information retention ability, their long-term memory, and take them closer to achieving their academic aspirations.

10

Passion

As you know, your child has greatness invested in them; they have the potential for that greatness to be unlocked; and they deserve to walk in their greatness and be fulfilled. What is greatness? Greatness is the state of being in the flow of your gifts and talents. Greatness requires mastery of your gifts and talents to serve others with excellence and – the key point of this chapter – with passion. Therefore, if you are to empower and support your child to unlock their greatness, you must first identify their passion.

Every child has a passion. And as a parent or educator, you have a duty and responsibility to discover what that is for your child. But, as we touched on earlier in the book, before you can do this, you need to ensure that you, too, are walking in your passion; that you, too, are walking in your greatness.

Do you know what your greatness is? Are you walking in it?

It is easy to recognise somebody who is walking in greatness. Have you ever been in a situation where you were dealing with two people doing the same job, with the same qualifications, the same level of experience, maybe even the same background? For example, you're looking for a tradesperson or professional of some sort, and you've found two people with equivalent credentials who could do the job. The only difference between them is that one is dedicated to their job but has no passion for it; the other is clearly passionate about their work, they are not merely trying to pay their bills each month. Which would you choose? The one who is keen to undercut their competitors and win another job or the one with a higher calling: to make a difference to someone else's life – to your life?

When you walk with passion in greatness, you are never in any competition. Your greatness is your greatest asset. It is what makes you stand out. Greatness is your USP and passion is your key to success.

Why is passion important?

Greatness and passion combined are the outworking of your purpose. Your purpose is your answer to the question, 'Why am I here?' You are here to serve. Your purpose must never be self-seeking, but always directed toward other people, toward future generations. You should always be asking yourself: 'How can I make a difference? How can I add value to other people's lives, to society? How can I make a lasting impact?'

As we have seen, many people are engaged in a job or a business that they do not enjoy. They don't enjoy it because they find no meaning in what they are doing. They work in this job because it pays well or is stress-free, but it gives them no fulfilment. Whether employment or entrepreneurship, doing what you are passionate about enables you to focus your attention and care on other people and means that, because you are walking in your greatness, there will be no stress. Yes, you will have challenging days in your career – that goes without saying – but you will have a sense of fulfilment, as this is what you have been called to do. If passion is missing, challenges at work will diminish your engagement, motivation and performance – not to mention your wellbeing.

When I interview prospective employees, I always ask the why question. I want people with passion, because the children I am responsible for always speak most highly of staff who have passion. Passion brings your gifts and talents out into the open and gives them life. From today, make it your mission to ignite that passion in your life and in your child's life. Think of a gas cooker. To light it, you must hold a match or lighter to something that is not visible – gas. It is the same with a child's potential. It may not be visible, but it is always there. It is your responsibility to ignite it so that they can walk in their greatness and live a fulfilled life. So that they won't be excluded or suspended from school, so that they won't become NEET. So that they too can make a generational impact, because they will have found their passion, which will drive them. When they are walking in their greatness, they will have no time to get into trouble, because they will be absorbed in doing what they were born to do.

But how do you discover what this is? How do you identify your child's gifts and talents? How do you unleash their passion?

Finding your child's passion

This task requires you to be sober-minded and vigilant. You need to engineer a situation, an environment in which your child is encouraged to discover their gifts and talents. An environment where they are allowed to find their flow, where they are praised for being in flow, where their behaviour is affirmed and they understand that it is good to self-actualise. You must instil a can-do mindset; this will empower your child to achieve.

Five ways to discover what your child is passionate about and nurture that passion are to:

1. Encourage your child to keep a journal, where they document what excites them and what

challenges them. Over time, you may see a pattern emerging.

2. Discuss with your child what is important to them (and what is not), to help clarify their values.

3. Note when your child is doing an activity that energises them, that excites them, when they are 'in the zone'. This will be signalled by time passing quickly for them.

4. Make resources available that relate to the passion they have revealed and that will help them to grow their passion.

5. Enrol your child in classes and educational programmes relating to their passion.

Summary

Passion drives performance. It determines engagement. It defines wellbeing. Walking in your greatness is not a journey with a destination; it is a lifestyle. It is a state of being, of being passionate about what you do. It is essential for you to identify and nurture both your own and your child's passion. Observe and talk to your child to uncover what they are passionate about, then identify ways in which you can nurture their passion.

11

Path

We are all walking down a path. The path represents our life. The path you are walking down now was either shown to you by default or chosen by you. Are you walking along your path by choice or by default? Following a path, a career, because you were told to may seem like the easier option, but in the long run it is the worst thing you can do. Following a default path that you haven't chosen for yourself will impact you later in life in ways that you never imagined possible.

It is imperative that your child follows a path that they choose. Since their development is shaped in and by their home environment, it is imperative that as parents you empower your child, that you do not dictate or impose a path on them, but rather support them to find their own path. Help them to find a path that will lead them to happiness and fulfilment, that will enable them to walk in their greatness.

You are aiming to help them get to a place where time disappears. In this place, there is an overwhelming excitement, joy, and sense of fulfilment from being in the flow of your gifts and talents, from knowing that you are walking in your greatness and having an impact in the world. This is the place you must help your child to find, the place where their path should lead.

The occupational and vocational paradigms

Along the path we call life are two paradigms: the occupational paradigm and the vocational paradigm. I've briefly mentioned these earlier in the book. As the name suggests, the occupational paradigm concerns how we occupy our time. The mindset of somebody living in an occupational paradigm is concerned with how they can generate an income to maintain a particular lifestyle. For example, the average salary in the UK is around £30,000 a year.[114] If you are in the occupational paradigm you will be asking the question, either consciously or subconsciously, 'What career should I choose, that will pay me £30,000 per annum, £2,500 a month, £600 a week, £120 a (working) day, £15 an hour?' While this may seem a rational approach, the danger is that we choose a career path purely because it pays what we perceive to be the required salary.

A typical indicator that somebody is in an occupational paradigm is that, for them, Monday is the worst day of the week – particularly at 6am when their alarm goes off. Similarly, Friday is the best day of the week, because the next day is Saturday, the start of the weekend and two days without work. Two days when they can do something enjoyable and fulfilling. For people in the occupational paradigm, they are constantly counting down to the next day off, the next weekend, the next holiday.

There is a better way: the vocational paradigm. The word vocation comes from the Latin *vocare*, which means 'to call'. A vocation is a calling and so is deeply connected with your gifts and talents and aligned with your purpose. Somebody who is living according to a vocational paradigm will be asking themselves, 'How can I serve? How can I make a lasting difference? How can I make an impact in this world?' An indicator that someone is in a vocational paradigm is that they are never wishing time away. Unlike those living in the occupational paradigm, Monday is the best day of the week, full of joy and excitement about doing what they were born to do.

Everyone should be living in the vocational paradigm, so encourage your child to pursue a path by choice, not by default.

Purpose of education

We often hear that young people have pursued a degree of some kind, only to find that they are unable to find a job or a business where that degree can be utilised, or that they cannot even identify a job or business that relates to the degree they have spent thousands of pounds obtaining. This is because they have started at the wrong end of their life path. It is essential to begin with the end in mind. This requires an awareness of what your child's talent is. Education is a tool that can and should be used to further refine your child's talents and help them to identify early on a path that aligns with them.

CHARLES

Charles (not his real name) joined our programme because his school had reported that he was underachieving and causing low-level disruption in class. His mother would frequently receive calls from the school about his behaviour and was constantly worrying. Charles also had challenges around socialising with children of his own age.

Charles has since made huge strides. We devised a learning strategy and coaching programme that helped both him and the school to improve his behaviour. His recent school reports have also shown a massive improvement in performance and he is now on track to pass his SATS. His mother is relieved that she is no longer receiving phone calls and being summoned to the school to discuss Charles's misbehaviour, and she enjoys a better relationship with her son.

In Chapter 3, I used the diamond analogy. No diamond was ever created in its full, polished form. Its beauty is incrementally brought out by the diamond miner, then by the jeweller who knows how to polish the diamond and cut it to reveal the beauty within. Your child must be similarly worked to bring out their greatness, which must be developed and refined. Education is the tool they need. The word education comes from two Latin words: *educere*, meaning 'to lead out' or bring out, and *educare*, meaning to mould or shape. Education is not simply a means of obtaining a degree or other qualification; it is a tool to lead your child toward the right path for them. True education is not a destination, but rather a journey; it is the training ground to bring out their gifts and talents to develop through mastery to excellence.

Financial literacy and wealth

Financial education has recently come into the spot-light, due to research finding that children from low socioeconomic status backgrounds are more suscep-tible to malnutrition, teenage pregnancy, educational underachievement, and physical and mental health challenges. Financial education is designed to address poverty by supporting children, young people and adults to develop the knowledge, skills and confidence necessary to escape poverty and, eventually, eradicate it altogether.[115]

The challenge we face is that children and young people tend to replicate what they see, including what their parents do in their formative years.[116] It is therefore incumbent upon us parents to give our children a financial education, to help them become 'financially literate' by furnishing them with the knowledge, skills and confidence to make sound financial decisions that will help them to build wealth and progress smoothly down their life path.

Of course, there is more to wealth than financial security and comfort. We tend to think of wealth purely in financial terms, as having lots of money, a big house, a nice car and so on. But true wealth is the ability to provide value to a person who needs your service. Your focus at work should never be on job security and earning potential, but on making yourself invaluable. Adding value makes you irreplaceable. This is the real principle of wealth that you should be instilling in your child and that will in turn lay the foundations for financial security throughout their life path.

Summary

We all have a path that is unique to us, based on our greatness, which emerges from our talent. Our path is our opportunity to stand out, to be seen and known for our greatness, to become irreplaceable. We must have the courage to pursue our talent and our calling by following the path we choose for ourselves, not the one that is envisioned for or expected of us. If we are on the right path, we should be living in a vocational paradigm. Education can help to ensure that your child follows the right path, provided they start with the end in mind. As well as academic education, financial education can also keep your child on the right path, by helping them to avoid the trappings of an occupational paradigm. The world is crying out for people to take the plunge and acknowledge and follow their talents. To make a dent, to make a difference, to make an impact. This is what we must be encouraging, enabling, and supporting our children to do.

PART THREE

FROM STRUGGLE TO SUCCESS

Success is not determined solely by working hard. Success is determined by applying the right principles. Being aware of these principles, knowing how to apply them strategically and developing a mindset that enables you to make the right decisions, will bring success.

To unlock the potential in your child so that they will be successful and have the career they deserve, so that they will walk in their greatness, be your legacy and leave their own and, most importantly, be fulfilled and happy, they require:

1. An empowering mindset

2. An effective learning strategy

3. A supportive environment.

This part of the book will show you how to provide all three of these.

12

An Empowering Mindset

Ancient literature states 'as a man thinks in his heart, so is he.' A belief is what we think and accept to be true; a mindset is a set of beliefs. What are your beliefs around success? More importantly, what are your child's beliefs around success? These beliefs will determine their experiences in the world, because the world we live in reflects our inner world.

As mentioned earlier in the book, we can approach life in one of two ways. We can adopt an inside-out approach, where we are validated by our inner world, which gives life to our outer world. Or, we can choose to live outside-in, where the outer world gives validation to our inner world. The danger of living outside-in is that people, circumstances and resources beyond our control come to determine our success, self-esteem and our wealth. This can have a long-term impact on how we see ourselves, and on our attitudes to work and personal development.

If we choose to live inside-out, we come to understand that everything that happens in our life is a result of our inner world, the result of our thoughts turned into beliefs. We hold these beliefs at a conscious level and, in turn, they manifest at a subconscious level, in our mindset, which will produce a corresponding result. This is the law of cause and effect in action. We reap what we sow. If we do not like the effects we are seeing in our life, we must go back to the cause: our mindset. Change our mindset and we change the result, giving us the success that we are looking for.

MINDSET → ACTION(S) → RESULT ─┬→ HEALTH
                                            ├→ RELATIONSHIPS
                                            ├→ EXAM RESULTS
                                            └→ FINANCES

The key is that there must be congruence between our mindset and our actions to give us the outcome we are looking to achieve. For your child, this could be better results in examinations, greater confidence, setting and achieving their goals, an improvement in learning strategies...Whatever it is they are looking for, if they can establish the appropriate mindset they will achieve the desired result. Your role here is to participate in cocreating an empowering environment; this will significantly improve the mindset of your child and will have a positive and long-lasting impact on their learning and performance.

Building an empowering mindset

The word 'empower' implies the ability to reach one's full potential. 'Potential' is the capacity to develop or become something that will lead to success. As such, when we talk about an empowering mindset, we are talking about a mindset that is conducive to success.

The difference between a child who is successful in their endeavours and a child who isn't is the mindset that they have adopted. A child who displays an empowering mindset believes that they can succeed and they adopt methods that will support this. A child with an empowering mindset understands that achieving success is about believing in your ability to succeed. This belief, this mindset, enables them to adopt the right learning strategies to unlock their potential. The grades and results they consequently achieve reinforce the belief that they have adopted the right methodology.

How do we build an empowering mindset? There are six requirements:

1. Adopt an inside-out approach to life.

2. Believe that intelligence can grow.

3. Treat success or failure as feedback to help inform your next steps.

4. Believe that it is your right to be successful.

5. Focus on the process, not the destination; in other words, look to improve your process of learning, rather than the results you achieve.

6. Seek to improve yourself.

Without an empowering mindset, a child is at risk of underachievement. Underachievement in a school environment is when a child achieves below their learning potential. This can be due to their self-concept, which is reflected in their behaviour. The beliefs they hold about themselves will determine not only their actions (or lack of), but the results they attain.[117]

Belief and intelligence

Those who have cultivated a disempowering mindset believe that their intellectual abilities are predetermined and there is nothing they can do to improve their intelligence. Their self-concept is skewed by the limiting belief that they are incapable of learning. This is because they repeatedly encounter learning experiences that are unpleasant and do not learn the skills necessary to navigate challenges, leaving them feeling frustrated. This leads to a downward spiral of repeated assessment results that do not reflect their ability, consequent anxiety associated with assessments, and fear of failure.[118]

Without doubt, these beliefs and perceptions will be deeply rooted in their past achievement and reinforcement history. Yet it is these subjective convictions about oneself, once established, that play a determining role in an individual's further growth and development,[119] and there is a strong relationship between self-concept and achievement.[120]

Science suggests that intelligence is changeable, thanks to the phenomenon of neuroplasticity, and those who adopt an empowering mindset believe that their intellectual abilities can be cultivated and developed through application. While people may differ in their starting skill levels, everyone can improve their underlying ability.[121] We all have potential for greatness, but it must be cultivated. Intelligence can only be improved through the application of an effective learning strategy and a positive support network, which will place your child in good stead to be trained to develop their intelligence – irrespective of any neurodiversity.[122] All success, including academic success, is the compound effect of applying the principles that govern success.

Self-efficacy

Psychologist Albert Bandura coined the term 'self-efficacy' to refer to a belief in one's ability to be successful, irrespective of the circumstances one finds oneself in, and in one's capability to assemble and implement the behaviours necessary to support future results.[123,124]

Perceived self-efficacy is a good indicator of a person's thoughts, emotions and actions.[125] It is important that parents, educators and policymakers develop and maintain an environment where children and young people's self-efficacy is positively cultivated; that we give them the tools necessary to better themselves. The secret to helping a child raise their attainment is to help cultivate an empowering mindset; this will increase their self-efficacy, as they will believe they can improve their skills and abilities to achieve success. We must empower children by instilling in them the unshakeable conviction and expectation that they will achieve their goals because they have the necessary skills, knowledge and abilities to do so.

Self-efficacy beliefs govern not only how children perceive prospects and hindrances, and consequently their choices, but also how much they are willing to strive and persist to be successful, and are shaped by four 'inputs':[126]

1. **Own experience.** Our prior experience of a particular task (known as enactive mastery experience) is the most reliable source of information for efficacy beliefs. Successes strengthen self-efficacy, whereas repeated failures weaken it. A firm sense of efficacy based on the evidence of past successes – especially those that presented a challenge and required effort and persistence – will help us to withstand temporary failures.[127] Yet a child's sense of self-efficacy can be damaged if they only achieve things effortlessly.[128]

2. **Vicarious experience.** We also establish
   self-efficacy beliefs based on other people's
   performance of similar tasks. This is known as
   vicarious experience or modelling. Vicarious
   experience has a greater influence on the
   formation of self-efficacy beliefs when there
   are no absolute measures of adequacy or
   competence.[129]

3. **Verbal persuasion.** Persuasive communication
   and evaluative feedback from others also
   influence our judgement of our self-efficacy.
   Verbal persuasion is most effective when
   those doing the persuading are considered
   knowledgeable and trustworthy. However,
   if one's own enactive mastery experience is
   negative, this can outweigh self-efficacy beliefs
   created solely based on verbal persuasion.

4. **Physiological reactions.** Heightened
   physiological effects such as sweating,
   accelerated heartbeat, fatigue, aches and pains,
   and mood changes can also affect our efficacy
   appraisal.

Parents, educators and policymakers have a duty to
ensure that these four inputs are empowering and
not disempowering for the children in their care. We
need to ensure that our child's experience of learning is positive, irrespective of their background and
characteristics. Neurodiversity needs to be embraced.
Every child is destined for greatness if furnished with

a positive support network, an effective learning strategy and an empowering mindset. Academic failure is often attributed to low capability, lack of trying[130] or internal causes.[131] It is therefore critical we work with all children, including and perhaps especially those who are neurodiverse, to develop a winning attitude, as this has been proven to positively influence their learning outcome and results.[132] We must also ensure that children are exposed to positive vicarious learning experiences, and that they meet, talk to and read about people who have achieved despite learning difficulties.

Above all, we must realise that there is power in the words we speak. I have witnessed many times adults speaking disempowering words to children; it is no wonder these children have extremely low perceived self-efficacy. What words are you speaking to your child, are they empowering or disempowering? If it's the latter, make a conscious decision to reverse this. Finally, we must do what we can to help children feel relaxed and anxiety-free in their learning environment, so that they are not disempowered by adverse physiological reactions.

A positive self-concept and high perceived self-efficacy are the essential components of an empowering mindset, which will lead to greater academic engagement and intrinsic motivation to learn, because the child believes that they can achieve.[133] A child with high perceived self-efficacy has good emotional wellbeing and will tend to work through challenges without giving up.[134] Frustration is a strong indicator that a child is not in their learning flow; a child with positive self-efficacy will experience few learning frustrations.

Summary

Academic success does not discriminate. It requires only diligence, tenacity and consistency. If you want to see your child fulfilled, successful and transformed, you must help them to develop an empowering mindset that will enable them to move past any previous challenges and/or limiting self-beliefs. They must believe in their own intelligence and self-efficacy, which is affected by their experiences – both personal and vicarious – and by the words that are spoken to them. An empowering mindset will break the cycle of underachievement, frustration, low self-esteem and negative self-efficacy, allowing your child to enter their learning flow, achieve academic success and walk in their greatness.

13

An Effective Learning Strategy

I'll begin this chapter with some interesting statistics. The first is that we retain only 5% of the information we hear in a learning environment – for example, a classroom, lecture or webinar. The second is that we retain only 10% of what we read.[135] As you can see, our retention of information is exceptionally low. This means that, if all your child does is go to school, listen to their teachers and read books, they will struggle when it comes to assessments. Every child needs a learning strategy, this is essential – but not just any learning strategy, an empowering learning strategy. In this chapter, we'll discover the difference between a disempowering and an empowering learning strategy.

Disempowering learning strategy

As the name suggests, a disempowering learning strategy is one that will prevent your child from reaching their full potential because the methods it uses will provide only short-term, ad hoc and temporary results. A disempowering learning strategy tends to involve:

- Cramming

- Test anxiety

- Hard work with poor results

Why are these methods disempowering? Let us consider each in turn.

Cramming

This is a method born out of an innate human desire to do well, in this case in exams and academia. Juggling schoolwork and other commitments can lead to neglect of the study habits that are most conducive to exam success, specifically a robust studying strategy. When there is no review of information and consolidation of knowledge, there is little chance of exam success. This is often compensated for by cramming.

Cramming is concentrated, focused study immediately before an exam.[136] It is a procrastination tactic; the work that should be done progressively is put off until a few days before the exam. It is a disempowering and ineffective learning strategy, but there are several possible reasons why your child might use it:

- Your child has not discovered their learning flow, where learning takes place effortlessly 'as a man thinks in his heart, so is he'.[137] If this is the case, it is essential that you empower them to discover their learning flow so that they do not resort to cramming.

- Your child has poor time management. In this case, you must support your child to manage their time more effectively. When developing a study routine, ensure that there is time for socialising, downtime and exercise – physical exercise is proven to support a healthier mind[138] and improve attention.[139]

- Your child lacks resources. To be successful in an exam, you need the necessary information. Does your child have all the information they need to do well? If your child is studying for GCSEs, find out what exam board is setting the examinations and ensure they have access to past papers and appropriate revision materials.

Working through the night before an exam may seem a good idea if time has run out and there is still work to be done, but sleep is essential for academic success (see Chapter 7). We need sleep to consolidate memories. If your child is sleep-deprived, they will be unable to consolidate their learning for easy recall when needed. This can lead to mental block in the exam, with disastrous consequences.

At best, cramming is a short-term fix. It will not empower your child to remember information in the long term; it will not develop their capacity for remembering nor their ability to synthesise and organise information.

Test anxiety

Test anxiety is distress at the thought of an exam, or anything associated with exams. Every child should be able to prepare for and sit exams free from anxiety. Unfortunately, 16.4% of UK secondary children suffer from test anxiety every year,[140] and the situation worsens with age: roughly 20% of sixth form and college students admit feeling test anxiety[141] and 25% of undergraduate students report having experienced it.[142] Not surprisingly, test anxiety is known to significantly harm exam performance.[143]

Test anxiety can arise due to poor historical academic performance.[144] For example, if Sophie is aiming to achieve Grade 4 in an exam but achieved only Grade 2 in her mock exam, it is likely she will experience test anxiety. It should be noted that test anxiety is more common in girls than boys[145] and in children with SEN.[146] From a psychological perspective, test anxiety results from fear of failure or of an inability to succeed, with inner thoughts like: 'I can't do this', 'I'm a failure', 'I'm not good enough', 'I'm not intelligent'. Such thoughts are symptoms of a disempowering mindset. A child with an empowering mindset will instead think: 'I can do this; I will be OK.' Empowering thoughts build emotional resilience and a positive outlook, the basis for positive outcomes – such as exam success. It is thus critical that parents, educators and policymakers alike support children and young people to cultivate empowering thoughts and the self-belief necessary for exam success.

Hard work with poor results

There is no alternative to hard work in delivering exam success, but what exactly do we mean by 'hard' work?

Picture a pair of trees. These are old, dying trees that need to be cut down and two people have been tasked with the felling, Person A and Person B. Person A exerts a lot of energy and it takes them two hours to cut down the tree, while Person B cuts down the tree in fifteen minutes with little energy exerted. How did Person B achieve this? They used a sharper axe. Person A started cutting without any preparation – a disempowering strategy – while Person B took the time to sharpen their axe – an empowering strategy.

Working hard while using a disempowering learning strategy will not result in grades that match your child's learning potential. They need an empowering learning strategy that is aligned with their unique learning flow and will therefore accelerate the unlocking of their learning potential. Preparedness is essential to academic success; to be adequately prepared, your child needs an empowering learning strategy with which to sharpen their axe.

Empowering learning strategy

As its name suggests, an empowering learning strategy is one designed to help your child reach their full potential and walk in their greatness. Bear in mind that every child is different, with a unique blend of gifts and talents, so their strategies will be different. Most importantly, an effective learning strategy empowers your child to work smart, not hard.

Establishing an empowering learning strategy starts with the question, 'What do I want to achieve?' You must always begin with the desired end in mind. For example, a child wanting to achieve a Grade 9 will adopt a different learning strategy from a child wanting to achieve a Grade 3. Goal-setting informs and drives the behavioural changes that will support learning.

An empowering strategy is concerned not merely with the *how*, but also with the *why*. Why does your child want to achieve this goal? Why do they value it? What is important to them? What motivates them? Being clear on these things will enable you to design an empowering learning strategy that will unlock your child's greatness.

Summary

Learning strategies can be either empowering or disempowering. Disempowering learning strategies will limit your child's achievement, as they can provide only short-term results and are highly inefficient, characterised by cramming and hard but unfocused work. This commonly arises out of test anxiety but does nothing to alleviate it. Without an empowering learning strategy, your child will not flourish – academically, or in life in general. They will miss opportunities and struggle to reach their full potential. For them to enjoy and make the most of the opportunities that await them, to have a career they are passionate about, they need an educational passport for progression. This requires an empowering learning strategy. This involves focused and consistent study with a clear goal in mind, adapted to the learning style and aims of your child.

14

A Supportive Environment

For every effect there is a cause. The household environment, as well as their wider community and social networks, are the causes that will shape your child's behaviour (effect). All parents are responsible for ensuring that the home environment is conducive to their child's learning and personal development, but there are other external factors and influences affecting your child's behaviour and progress that need to be accounted for also.

Peer pressure

According to Webster's Dictionary, peer pressure is 'a feeling that one must do the same things as other people of one's age and social group in order to be liked or respected by them.'[147]

The statistics on peer pressure are alarming. According to a recent publication:[148]

- Only 10% of teenagers said that they had never experienced peer pressure.

- 23% of teenage girls and 33% of boys felt pressured to have sex.

- 70% of teens who smoked said they started because friends smoked or pressured them to try it.

- 55% of teens tried drugs for the first time because they felt pressured to by their friends.

We have a duty to ensure that the children in our care – whether that's in our household or work environment – are empowered to develop a healthy self-concept – a positive image of who they are. Children and young people are more vulnerable to peer pressure when their self concept is weak, and will tend to behave in a way that enables them to fit in and feel respected, rather than in a way that will enable them to reach their potential and achieve greatness. Our achievements depend on our self-concept. If we like and respect ourselves, we are internally validated and do not need external validation from others, which is what makes people vulnerable to peer pressure.

Peer pressure is at its strongest during Key Stage transitions, and particularly during the transition between

Years 6 and 7, when adolescence begins. During this time, children become more aware of themselves and of others and feel a need to belong to a group to develop their identity. It is thus critical that parents, educators and policymakers put in place systems and practices to ensure that we can be a support to children and young people.

As a parent, the key strategies that will minimise negative peer pressure are to:

- Build strong family values
- Reduce your child's exposure to negative influences
- Investigate the community settings your child is entering, including their circle of friends

Let's look at each of these in turn.

Family values

In a world of so much technological advancement, it amazes me how life can remain busy. This makes it even more necessary to be strategic in carving time out of your busy schedule to spend with your family, for example, putting time aside for annual holidays, creating daily family times (eg breakfast and dinner time), or a weekly block of time together to gel. It is not necessarily the quantity of time spent together as a family, but the quality of that time. Positive interaction with your children in this time will build emotional resilience, as you model great character and empower your child(ren) with problem-solving skills, supporting them in overcoming challenges.

An important focus of quality time with your child(ren) should be to help build and strengthen their moral compass by imparting sound principles. A compass enables leadership by showing you the direction you are travelling in; a strong moral compass will enable your child to be confident in the direction of their life path.

Negative influences

Often, children underachieve because they are associating with other underachievers and do not see anybody in their circle or environment who has achieved, or indeed values, greatness. It is therefore important for you to know who your child is associating with and steer them towards individuals and groups that will be a positive influence.

Community

Similarly, within your community, encourage your child to engage with positive, inspiring people rather than those who could instil negative thoughts and beliefs. A positive peer group is one in which your child will associate and make friends with other young people on the journey to greatness. They will share their experiences, their challenges and successes, and you will make friends with other parents who are similarly committed to unlocking the potential in their children. This is important – throughout my years of working with children in a variety of environments, I have noticed that parents can only unlock potential to the degree that they have unlocked their own.

We cannot be around our children twenty-four-seven, but it is important to know who your child's friends are and get to know them and their families. Who are your child's friends? Who is their best friend? If you don't know, find out today.

An empowering team

While we can see the damaging effects of negative peer pressure, not all peer pressure is bad. There are strategies that I recommend you use for creating positive peer pressure for your child and building an empowering team around them.

I treat 'team' as an acronym: Together Everyone Achieves More. In a team, everybody is working towards the same goal. In our context, that goal is greatness. Building an empowering team will help you to strengthen and leverage your combined efforts in unlocking the greatness invested in your child. An empowering team will generate positive peer pressure.

Positive peer pressure helps young people to achieve more, by observing others working hard to reach their goals and striving towards a positive end. Over time, this will begin to expose them to adults with strong values who are achieving great things in life, in terms of their careers and relationships, and who can share the strategies that have driven their success. By doing what you can to facilitate a positive peer group for your child, you will empower them to unlock their greatness.

No man is an island, and you cannot unlock your child's potential by yourself. You need support. Your empowering team could consist of you, as parent(s), your child's school, and perhaps professional assistance, for example a mentor or coach. For parents, a key cause of anxiety or fear is lack of knowledge. Building knowledge means building resilience, and to be empowering you need to be empowered yourself. By developing your own knowledge base, you will be enabled to make informed decisions for your child's future.

As we learned earlier in the book, one of the key reasons why children underachieve is because parents do not understand how to navigate the educational maze. They are not fully aware of how the education system works and the important milestones. By understanding and communicating with your child's school, you can bring them into your empowering team.

If you feel that your empowering team could be strengthened even further, or if your child could benefit from some personalised attention and targeted assistance, you could consider a mentor. There are six key benefits of utilising a mentor; they can help your child by enabling them to:

1. Develop a reflective practice

2. Understand their strengths and areas for development

3. Learn from the successes and failures of someone with more life experience

4. Acquire a springboard for encouragement

5. Obtain expert guidance on professional development

6. Improve their personal and academic performance

Summary

A supportive and empowering environment is critical to your child's success. As well as influences from their home environment and local community, they will also be exposed to peer pressure, which can be both a negative and a positive force. Strong family values will help them to resist negative peer pressure, but to be successful, your child also needs to see and feel supported by other successful people, to be exposed to a supportive environment in which they can observe success. Your child needs to be part of a positive community that believes they can achieve.

Conclusion

People never knew it was possible to build a craft that could fly until it happened. Nothing is possible until you perceive it to be so, until you see it with your mind's eye. This means that when you decide that a dream is possible, it becomes possible.

The purpose of education should be to 'see' the gifts, talents, passion and purpose in children and empower them to unlock their full potential. Unfortunately, this is often not the case. Too many children are leaving the education system underachieving. Fellow parents, educators and policymakers, it is time to change the narrative. It is time to see every child, irrespective of their learning disposition and socioeconomic background, achieve academic success, pursue a passion-driven career and lead happy, fulfilled and successful lives.

Having read this book, you should be ready to inspire the greatness invested in your child and ignite a movement of young people who are socially mobilised and make a positive contribution to society. I look forward to witnessing the impact you will make.

Acknowledgements

This book would have been impossible without the help, guidance and support of many extraordinary people.

Firstly, thank you Mum and Dad. You demonstrated how to 'see' potential in children and inspired me to be the person I am today.

Thank you to my amazing wife, Natalie. You have been incredible, and I am blessed to have you by my side. I am committed to you and to ensuring your potential is always unlocked. Love you always.

To my precious daughter, Princess aka Hannah. You are an absolute diamond. I am honoured to be your daddy. Love you always.

Thank you to my mentors, both present and former. Thank you Daniel Priestley, for teaching me the outstanding principles of how I can enhance my impact in this world through my gifts and talents.

Thank you to my brothers, sisters, family members and friends. You know who are you – thank you for being you.

Rethink Press, you are simply outstanding. You have made my journey to published author seamless: Joe G, Lucy, Anke, Kate and Joe L.

Thank you to all the children, young people and parents we have previously served and currently serve at Potential Unlocked. You are my absolute delight, and I am committed to Inspire Your Greatness.

And finally, thank you to you – the reader. For picking up and reading this book and putting you and your child on a path which I know will result in phenomenal transformation to fulfilment and success.

Resources

The Inspire Your Greatness Scorecard

Want to score your ability to inspire your child's greatness?

The *Inspire Your Child's Greatness* Scorecard contains forty questions around the seven principles outlined in this book. You'll get a personalised report on your ability to unlock the potential in your children and how you can improve it. It's a great complementary tool to learn more about your capability to raise fulfilled, successful and transformed children.

To take the Inspire Your Greatness Scorecard test, visit https://inspireyourchildsgreatness.scoreapp.com

The Inspire Your Greatness Seminar

Ready to apply what you have read here? If so, why not take part in one of David's seminars?

Every year, David runs a number of one- and two-day seminars.

The Inspire Your Greatness seminar will empower you and your child to implement the 7 Inspire Your Child's Greatness Principles to leave you and your child feeling inspired, fulfilled and empowered to achieve a passion-driven career.

To find out more about our Inspire Your Child's Greatness seminar, please visit our website: https://davidchall.co.uk/see-me-live

Events

David is also a guest speaker at conferences and events and renowned for leaving the audience feeling inspired to lead fulfilled, successful and transformed lives. To find out more about David's events and/or book David for your conference or event, visit: www.davidchall.co.uk

References

1. Collins Dictionary, 'Maze', www.collinsdictionary.com/dictionary/english/maze
2. A Park, R Curtice, K Thomson, M Phillips and M Johnson, *British Social Attitudes, the 23rd Report: Perspectives on a changing society* (Sage, 2007)
3. N Lockwood, *Work/Life Balance: Challenges and solutions* (Society for Human Resource Management, 2003)
4. Wordspy, 'Work-Life Balance' (Wordspy, 2000) www.wordspy.com/words/work-lifebalance.asp
5. Gallup, *State of the Global Workplace – Gallup Report* (Gallup Inc, 2017)
6. C Ryff and C Keyes, 'The Structure of Psychological Well-being Revisited', *Journal of Personality and Social Psychology*, 69 (1995), 719–27, https://doi.org/10.1037//0022–3514.69.4.719
7. MD Newcomb and LL Harlow, 'Life Events and Substance Use Among Adolescents: Mediating effects of perceived loss of control and meaninglessness in life', *Journal of Personality and Social Psychology*, 51 (1986), 564–77
8. S Taylor, *Back to Sanity: Healing the madness of the human mind* (Hay House, 2012)
9. DH Pink, *Drive: The surprising truth about what motivates us* (Riverhead Books, 2009)
10. M Csikszentmihalyi, *Flow: The psychology of optimal experience* (Rider, 1990)
11. LL Harlow, MD Newcomb and PM Bentler, 'Depression, Self-degradation, Substance Use and Suicide Ideation', *Journal of Clinical Psychology*, 42/1(1986), 5–21
12. JE Crandall and RD Rasmussen, 'Purpose in Life as Related to Specific Values', *Journal of Individual Psychology*, 24 (1975), 74–81
13. NZ Hampton, 'The Relationship of Learning Disabilities to The Sources of Self-efficacy Expectations, and Academic Achievement in High School Students' Efficacy' (1996) (Order No. 9623977). Available from ProQuest Dissertations & Theses Global, Lexington, KY. (304312951)
14. CM Christensen, MB Horn and CW Johnson, *Disrupting Class: How disruptive innovation will change the way the world learns* (McGraw-Hill, 2008)

15. D Overbye, 'The New Einstein – Wait a Century' (New York Times, 2005) www.nytimes.com/2005/03/03/health/the-next -einstein-wait-a-century.html

16. M Kuhfeld, 'Surprising New Evidence on Summer Learning Loss', The Phi Delta Kappan, 101/1 (2019), 25–29, https://doi.org/10.1177 /0031721719871560

17. AM Ryan, 'The Peer Group as a Context for the Development of Young Adolescent Motivation and Achievement', *Child Development*, 72/4 (2003), 1135–1150 https://doi.org/10.1111/1467 –8624.00338

18. M Csikszentmihalyi, *Flow: The psychology of optimal experience* (Rider, 1990)

19. UK Government, *Ethnicity Facts and Figures* (Gov.uk, 2021) www .ethnicity-facts-figures.service.gov.uk/education-skills-and -training/11-to-16-years-old/a-to-c-in-english-and-maths-gcse -attainment-for-children-aged-14-to-16-key-stage-4/latest

20. Office for National Statistics, *ONS Labour Force Survey: Young people not in education, employment or training (NEET)* (ONS, 2020) www.ons.gov.uk/employmentandlabourmarket /peoplenotinwork/unemployment/bulletins/youngpeoplenotine ducationemploymentortrainingneet/august2020

21. B Coles, C Godfrey, A Keung, S Parrott and J Bradshaw, 'Estimating the Life-time Cost of NEET: 16–18-year-olds not in education, employment or training' (The Audit Commission, University of York, 2010) www.york.ac.uk/inst/spru/research/pdf /NEET.pdf

22. Prince's Trust, The Cost of Exclusion: Counting the cost of youth disadvantage in the UK (Prince's Trust, 2010) www.scie -socialcareonline.org.uk/the-cost-of-exclusion-counting-the-cost -of-youth-disadvantage-in-the-uk/r/a11G000000180V8IAI

23. *Average Household Income UK: Financial year 2020* (Gov.uk, 2021) www.ons.gov.uk/peoplepopulationandcommunity /personalandhouseholdfinances/incomeandwealth/bulletins /householddisposableincomeandinequality/financialyear2020

24. UK Government, *Households Below Average Income* (Gov.uk, 2013)

25. Audit Commission for Local Authorities and the National Health Service in England, *Against the Odds: Re-engaging young people in education, employment or training* (Audit Commission, 2010)

26. Ibid

27. Public Health England, *Local Action on Health Inequalities: Reducing the number of young people not in employment, education or training (NEET)* (Public Health England, 2014) https://assets.publishing .service.gov.uk/government/uploads/system/uploads/attachment _data/file/356062/Review3_NEETs_health_inequalities.pdf

28. K Bathgate and J Bird, *Identifying Young People at Risk of Becoming 'Not in Employment, Education or Training'* (Welsh Government, 2013)
29. B Francis-Devine, *Poverty in the UK: Statistics* (UK Parliament, 2021) https://commonslibrary.parliament.uk/research-briefings /sn07096/#:~:text=How%20many%20people%20are%20in,level %20to%20the%20year%20before
30. Public Health England, *Local Action on Health Inequalities*
31. S Maguire, 'Will Raising the Participation Age in England Solve the NEET Problem?' *Research in Post-Compulsory Education*, 18/1–2 (2013), 61–76
32. Public Health England, *Local Action on Health Inequalities*
33. C Taylor, *Improving Attendance at School* (DFE, 2012)
34. Department for Education, *The Link Between Absence and Attainment at KS2 and KS4 2013/14 Academic Year* (DFE, 2016)
35. S Maguire, 'Will Raising the Participation Age in England Solve the NEET Problem?'
36. Department for Education, *Permanent and Fixed-Period Exclusions in England: 2016 to 2017* (DFE, 2018) www.gov.uk/government /statistics/permanent-and-fixed-period-exclusions-in-england -2016-to-2017
37. UK Government, *Temporary Exclusions* (Gov.uk, 2021) www .ethnicity-facts-figures.service.gov.uk/education-skills-and -training/absence-and-exclusions/pupil-exclusions/latest
38. Department for Education, *Permanent and Fixed-Period Exclusions in England*
39. Department for Education, *Timpson Review of School Exclusion* (DFE, 2019) https://assets.publishing.service.gov.uk/government /uploads/system/uploads/attachment_data/file/807862/Timpson _review.pdf
40. Department for Education, *Exclusion from Maintained Schools, Academies and Pupil Referral Units in England* (DFE, 2017) https:// assets.publishing.service.gov.uk/government/uploads/system /uploads/attachment_data/file/921405/20170831_Exclusion_Stat _guidance_Web_version.pdf
41. Department for Education, *Special Educational Needs in England: January 2018* (DFE, 2018) https://assets.publishing.service.gov.uk /government/uploads/system/uploads/attachment_data/file /729208/SEN_2018_Text.pdf
42. Department for Education, *A Profile of Pupil Exclusions in England* (DFE, 2012) https://assets.publishing.service.gov.uk/government /uploads/system/uploads/attachment_data/file/183498/DFE -RR190.pdf
43. Department for Education, *Permanent and Fixed-Period Exclusions in England*

44. K Bathgate and J Bird, *Identifying Young People at Risk of Becoming 'Not in Employment, Education or Training'*

45. C Ajila and A Olutola, 'Impact of Parents' Socioeconomic Status on University Students' Academic Performance', *Ife Journal of Educational Studies*, 7 (2000), 31–39

46. OA Asikhia, 'Students and Teachers' Perception of the Causes of Poor Academic Performance in Ogun State Secondary Schools [Nigeria]: Implications for counselling for national development', *European Journal of Social Sciences*, 13 (2010), 229–249

47. OC Chukwudi, *Academic Performance of Secondary School Students: The effect of home environment* (Double Gist Publishers, 2013)

48. C Ajila and A Olutola, 'Impact of Parents' Socioeconomic Status on University Students' Academic Performance'

49. SE Rimm-Kaufman, RC Pianta, et al, 'Teacher Rated Family Involvement and Children's Social and Academic Outcomes in Kindergarten', *Early Education & Development*, 14 (2003), 179–198

50. R Koestne, M Zuckerman and J Koestner, 'Attributional Focus of Praise and Children's Intrinsic Motivation: The moderating role of gender', *Personality and Social Psychology Bulletin*, 15/1 (1989) 61–72, https://doi.org/10.1177/0146167289151006

51. EA Gunderson, SJ Gripshover, et al, 'Parent Praise to 1- to 3-year-olds Predicts Children's Motivational Frameworks 5 Years Later', *Child Development*, 84/5 (2013),1526–41

52. SR Zentall and BJ Morris, 'Good Job, You're So Smart: The effects of inconsistency of praise type on young children's motivation', *Journal of Experimental Child Psychology*, 107/2 (2010),155–63

53. CM Mueller and CSJ Dweck, 'Praise for Intelligence Can Undermine Children's Motivation and Performance', *Journal of Personality and Social Psychology*, 75/1 (1998), 33–52

54. K Christian, FJ Morrison and FB Bryant 'Predicting Kindergarten Academic Skills: Interactions among childcare, maternal education, and family literacy environments', *Early Childhood Research Quarterly*, 13 (1998), 501–521

55. Y Chida and A Steptoe, 'The Association of Anger and Hostility with Future Coronary Heart Disease: A meta-analytic review of prospective evidence', *J Am Coll Cardiol.* (2009) 53(11):936–46

56. LL Toussaint, GS Shields and GM Slavich, 'Forgiveness, Stress, and Health: A 5-Week Dynamic Parallel Process Study', *Ann Behav Med.* (2016) 50(5):727–735. doi: 10.1007/s12160-016-9796-6

57. CC Cottle, RJ Lee and K Heilbrun, 'The Prediction of Criminal Recidivism in Juveniles: A meta-analysis', *Criminal Justice and Behavior*, 28(3) (2001), 367–394

58. Collins Dictionary, *Empower*, www.collinsdictionary.com /dictionary/english/empower

59. B Verplanken and H Aarts, 'Habit, Attitude, and Planned Behaviour: Is habit an empty construct or an interesting case of

goal-directed automaticity?', *European Review of Social Psychology*, 10 (1999), 101–134

60. KR Arlinghaus and CA Johnston, 'The Importance of Creating Habits and Routine', *American Journal of Lifestyle Medicine*, 13/2 (2018), 142–144, http://doi.org/10.1177/1559827618818044

61. JA Bargh, 'The Four Horsemen of Automaticity: Awareness, intention, efficiency, and control in social cognition', In RS Wyer and TK Srull (Eds) *Handbook of Social Cognition: Vol 1 Basic Processes* (Lawrence Erlbaum Associates Publishers, 1994) 1–40

62. P Lally, CHM van Jaarsveld, et al, 'How are Habits Formed? Modelling habit formation in the real world', *European Journal of Social Psychology*, 40 (2010), 998–1009, doi:10.1002/ejsp.674

63. *Institute of Medicine Dietary Reference Intakes Macronutrients Report, 2002.*

64. O Bar-Or, R Dotan, et al, 'Voluntary Hypohydration in 10- to 12-year-old Boys', *Journal of Applied Physiology*, 48 (1980), 104–108

65. A Griffiths and S Ghezelayagh, *Children and Young People and Financial Capability: Needs analysis* (The Money Advice Service, 2018) https://moneyandpensionsservice.org.uk/wp-content /uploads/2021/03/cyp-needs-analysis.pdf

66. T Clarke and S Ghezelayagh, *Measuring Financial Capability in Children and Young People: What drives financial behaviour?* (The Money Advice Service, 2018) https://moneyandpensionsservice .org.uk/wp-content/uploads/2021/03/measuring-financial -capability-in_-children-and-young-people.pdf

67. K Black and M Lobo, 'A Conceptual Review of Family Resilience Factors', *Journal of Family Nursing*, 14 (2008), 33–55, http://doi.org /10.1177/1074840707312237

68. BH Fiese, TJ Tomcho, M Douglas, K Josephs, S Poltrock and T Baker, 'A review of 50 years of research on naturally occurring family routines and rituals: cause for celebration?', *Journal of Family Psychology*, 16 (2002), 381–390

69. M Spagnola and B Fiese, 'Family routines and rituals: A context for development in the lives of young children', *Infants & Young Children*, 20 (2007), 284–299

70. BH Fiese, T Tomcho, M Douglas, K Josephs, S Poltrock and T Baker, 'Fifty years of research on naturally occurring rituals: Cause for celebration?', *Journal of Family Psychology*, 16 (2002), 381–390

71. JA Mindell, ES Leichman, et al, 'Implementation of a Nightly Bedtime Routine: How quickly do things improve?', *Infant Behavior and Development*, 4 (2017), 220–227, http://doi.org/10.1016 /j.infbeh.2017.09.013

72. JA Mindell and AA Williamson, 'Benefits of a Bedtime Routine in Young Children: Sleep, development, and beyond', *Sleep Medicine Reviews*, 40 (2018), 93–108, http://doi.org/10.1016/j.smrv.2017.10.007

73. D Willingham, 'Are Sleepy Students Learning?' (American Educator, 2012–13) www.aft.org/pdfs/americaneducator/winter1213/willingham.pdf

74. R Dawkins, 'The Importance of Sleep for Kids' (Johns Hopkins Medicine, 2018) www.hopkinsallchildrens.org/ACH-News/General-News/The-importance-of-sleep-for-kids

75. V Dunckley, 'Wired and Tired: Electronics and sleep disturbance in children' (Psychology Today, 2011) https://www.psychologytoday.com/us/blog/mental-wealth/201103/wired-and-tired-electronics-and-sleep-disturbance-in-children

76. MM Garrison, K Liekweg and DA Christakis, 'Media Use and Child Sleep: The impact of content, timing, and environment', *Pediatrics*, 128/1 (2011), 29–35

77. DT Neal, W Wood, et al, 'How Do Habits Guide Behavior? Perceived and actual triggers of habits in daily life', *Journal of Experimental Social Psychology*, 48 (2012), 492–498, http://doi.org/10.1016/j.jesp.2011.10.011

78. L Aldabal and AS Bahammam, 'Metabolic, Endocrine, and Immune Consequences of Sleep Deprivation', *The Open Respiratory Medicine Journal*, 5 (2011), 31–43

79. MA Willgerodt and GM Kieckhefer, 'School Nurses Can Address Existing Gaps in School Age Sleep Research', *Journal of School Nursing*, 29/3 (2013), 175–180

80. J Ingwersen, MA Defeyter, et al, 'A Low Glycaemic Index Breakfast Cereal Preferentially Prevents Children's Cognitive Performance from Declining Throughout The Morning', *Appetite*, 49/1 (2007), 240–4

81. R Micha, PJ Rogers, M Nelson, 'Glycaemic Index and Glycaemic Load of Breakfast Predict Cognitive Function and Mood in School Children: A randomised controlled trial', *British Journal of Nutrition*, 106/10 (2011), 1552–61

82. NF Watson, MS Badr, et al, 'Recommended Amount of Sleep for a Healthy Adult: A Joint Consensus Statement of the American Academy of Sleep Medicine and Sleep Research Society', *Sleep* (2015) 38(6):843–4

83. S Moturi and K Avis, 'Assessment and Treatment of Common Pediatric Sleep Disorders', *Psychiatry*, 7/6 (2010), 24–37;

84. S Chiu, DA Nutter, et al, 'Pediatric Sleep Disorders Treatment and Management: Cognitive behavioral therapy' (Medscape, 2018) https://emedicine.medscape.com/article/916611-overview

85. MM Perfect, K Archbold, et al, 'Risk of Behavioral and Adaptive Functioning Difficulties in Youth with Previous and Current Sleep Disordered Breathing', *Sleep*, 36/4 (2013), 517–525

86. KA Bonuck, RD Chervin, et al, 'Prevalence and Persistence of Sleep Disordered Breathing Symptoms in Young Children: A 6-year population-based cohort study', *Sleep*, 34/7 (2011), 875–884

87. NF Watson et al, 'Recommended Amount of Sleep for a Healthy Adult: A joint consensus statement of the American Academy of Sleep Medicine and Sleep Research Society'

88. D Willingham, 'Are Sleepy Students Learning?' (American Educator, 2012) www.aft.org/sites/default/files/periodicals /Willingham_1.pdf

89. Office of Disease Prevention and Health Promotion, *Sleep Health* (United States Department of Health and Human Services, 2020) www.healthypeople.gov/2020/topicsobjectives2020/overview .aspx?topicid=38

90. NE Hill and SA Craft, 'Parent-school Involvement and School Performance: Mediated pathways among socioeconomically comparable African American and Euro-American families', *Journal of Educational Psychology*, 96 (2003), 74–83

91. A Henderson and K Mapp, 'A New Wave of Evidence: The impact of school, family, and community connections on student achievement', *Annual Synthesis* (Southwest Educational Development Laboratory, Texas, 2002)

92. C Jordan, E Orozco and A Averett, 'Emerging Issues in School, Family and Community Connections', *Annual Synthesis* (Southwest Educational Development Laboratory, Texas, 2001)

93. S Harter and R Pike, 'The Pictorial Scale of Perceived Competence and Social Acceptance for Young Children', *Child Development*, 55 (1984), 1969–1982

94. F Smit, H Moerel, K van der Wolf and P Sleegers, *Building Bridges Between Home and School* (ITS/SCO-Kohnstamm Instituut, 1999)

95. J Epstein, 'School/Family/Community Partnerships: Caring for the children we share', Phi Delta Kappan (1995), 701–712

96. NE Hill and SA Craft, 'Parent-school Involvement and School Performance: Mediated pathways among socioeconomically comparable African American and Euro-American families'

97. SE Rimm-Kaufman, RC Pianta, MJ Cox and MJ Bradley, 'Teacher Rated Family Involvement and Children's Social and Academic Outcomes in Kindergarten', *Early Education & Development*, 14 (2003), 179–198

98. T Kellaghan, K Sloane, B Alvarez and B Bloom, *The Home Environment and School Learning* (Jossey-Bass Publishers, 1993)

99. SH Birch and GW Ladd, 'The Teacher–Child Relationship and Children's Early School Adjustment', *Journal of School Psychology*, 35 (1997), 61–79

100. S Herculano-Houzel, 'The Remarkable, Yet Not Extraordinary, Human Brain as a Scaled-up Primate Brain and its Associated Cost', *Proceedings of the National Academy of Sciences of the United States of America*, 109/1 (2012), 10661–8, doi:10.1073/pnas .1201895109

101. H Koizumi, *The Scope of the Symposium 8th International Conference on Functional Mapping of the Human Brain*, June 2–6, Sendai, Japan (2002)

102. TH Bak, JJ Nissan, MM Allerhand and IJ Deary, 'Does Bilingualism Influence Cognitive Aging?', *Annals of Neurology*, 75 (2014), 959–963, https://doi.org/10.1002/ana.24158

103. H Koizumi, 'Science of Learning and Education: An approach with brain-function imaging', *No To Hattatsu*, 35/2 (2003), 126–129

104. BN Macnamara, DZ Hambrick and FL Oswald, 'Deliberate Practice and Performance in Music, Games, Sports, Education, and Professions: A meta-analysis', *Psychological Science*, 25 (2014), 1608–1618. doi:10.1177/09567976145 35810

105. KA Ericsson, RTH Krampe and C Tesch-Römer, 'The Role of Deliberate Practice in The Acquisition of Expert Performance', *Psychological Review*, 100 (1993), 363–406, https://graphics8.nytimes.com/images/blogs/freakonomics/pdf/DeliberatePractice(PsychologicalReview).pdf

106. 'Brainwaves – the definitions', no date, Neurohealth.com, https://nhahealth.com/brainwaves-the-language

107. JW Pennebaker and ME Francis, 'Cognitive, Emotional, and Language Processes in Disclosure', *Cognition and Emotion*, 10 (1996), 601–626

108. K Klein and A Boals, 'Expressive Writing can Increase Working Memory Capacity', *Journal of Experimental Psychology: General*, 130 (2001), 520–533

109. G Ramirez and SL Beilock, 'Writing About Testing Worries Boosts Exam Performance in the Classroom', *Science*, 331 (2011), 211–213, http://doi.org/10.1126/science.1199427

110. JW Pennebaker and A Graybeal, 'Patterns of Natural Language Use: Disclosure, personality, and social integration', *Current Directions*, 10 (2001), 90–93

111. KA Baikie and K Wilhelm, 'Emotional and Physical Health Benefits of Expressive Writing', *Advances in Psychiatric Treatment*, 11/5 (2005), 338–346, doi:10.1192/apt.11.5.338

112. Coffield, 'It Takes Two to Tango' (Paper written upon request of CERI in preparation of the 4th meeting of the CERI's Lifelong Learning Network), Wako-shi, 2004

113. J Sweller, 'Cognitive Load Theory', *Psychology of Learning and Motivation*, 55 (2011), 37–76

114. Office for National Statistics, *Average Household Income, UK: Financial year 2020* (ONS, 2021) www.ons.gov.uk/peoplepopulationandcommunity/personalandhouseholdfinances/incomeandwealth/bulletins/householddisposableincomeandinequality/financialyear2020

115. Child and Youth Finance International (CYFI), *Training Course on Fostering National Financial Education Strategies* (Podgorica: CYFI and GIZ, 2016)

116. AMC Otto, *The Economic Psychology of Adolescent Saving* (doctoral thesis, University of Exeter, 2009)

117. AA Attwell, 'Some Factors That Contribute to Underachievement in School: A suggested remedy', *Elementary School Guidance & Counseling*, 3/2 (1968), 98–103

118. CS Dweck, *Self-theories: Their role in motivation, personality, and development* (Psychology Press, 1999)

119. A Bandura, *Self-efficacy: The exercise of control* (W.H. Freeman, 1997)

120. X Ma and N Kishor, 'Attitude Toward Self, Social Factors, and Achievement in Mathematics: A meta-analytic view', *Educational Psychology Review*, 9 (1997), 89–120

121. CS Dweck, *Self-theories*

122. CS Dweck, *Mindsets and Math/Science Achievement* (The Opportunity Equation, 2014) www.growthmindsetmaths .com/uploads/2/3/7/7/23776169/mindset_and_math_science _achievement_-_nov_2013.pdf

123. A Bandura, *Social Foundations of Thought and Action: A social cognitive theory* (Prentice-Hall, 1986)

124. A Bandura, *Social Learning Theory* (Prentice-Hall, 1977)

125. M Bong and E Skaalvik, 'Academic Self-concept and Self-efficacy: How different are they really?', *Educational Psychology Review*, 15 (2003), 1–40

126. A Bandura, *Social Foundations of Thought and Action: A social cognitive theory* (Prentice-Hall, 1986)

127. M Bong and E Skaalvik, 'Academic Self-concept and Self-efficacy: How different are they really?'

128. A Bandura, *Self-efficacy in Changing Societies* (Cambridge University Press, 1995)

129. DH Schunk and AE Hanson, 'Peer models: Influence on children's self-efficacy and achievement', *Journal of Educational Psychology*, 77/3 (1985), 313–322, https://psycnet.apa.org/doiLanding?doi=10 .1037%2F0022-0663.77.3.313

130. B Weiner, 'An Attributional Theory of Achievement Motivation and Emotion', *Psychological Review*, 92/4 (1985), 548–573

131. TH Bryan, 'Self-concept and Attributions of the Learning Disabled', *Learning Disabilities Focus*, 1/2 (1986), 82–89

132. CS Dweck, *Mindset: The new psychology of success* (Random House, 2006)

133. CM Christensen, MB Horn and CW Johnson, *Disrupting Class: How disruptive innovation will change the way the world learns (Vol. 98)* (McGraw-Hill, 2008)

134. BJ Zimmerman, 'Self-efficacy: An essential motive to learn', *Contemporary Educational Psychology*, 25 (2000), 82–91, https://doi .org/10.1006/ceps.1999.1016

135. E Dale, *Audiovisual Methods in Teaching* (Dryden Press, 1969)

136. R Sommer, 'The Social Psychology of Cramming', *Personnel and Guidance Journal*, 9 (1968), 104–109

137. Proverbs 23:7, King James Verson (KJV)

138. CH Hillman, KI Erickson and AF Kramer, 'Be Smart, Exercise Your Heart: Exercise effects on brain and cognition', *Nature Reviews Neuroscience*, 9/1(2008), 58–65

139. JB Bartholomew and EM Jowers, 'Physically Active Academic Lessons in Elementary Children', *Preventive Medicine*, 52/1 (2011), 51–54

140. D Putwain and AL Daly, 'Test Anxiety Prevalence and Gender Differences in a Sample of English Secondary School Students', *Educational Studies*, 40 (2014), 554–570, https://doi.org/ 10.1080/03055698.2014.953914

141. T Ergene, 'Effective Interventions on Test Anxiety Reduction: A meta-analysis', *School Psychology International*, 24 (2003), 313–328, https://doi.org/10.1177/01430343030243004

142. CL Thomas, JC Cassady and WH Finch, 'Identifying Severity Standards on the Cognitive Test Anxiety Scale: Cut score determination using latent class and cluster analysis', *Journal of Psychoeducational Assessment*, 36 (2018), 492–508

143. S Chamberlain, AL Daly and V Spalding, 'The Fear Factor: Students' experiences of test anxiety when taking A-level examinations', *Pastoral Care in Education*, 29/3 (2011), 193–205

144. N von der Embse, D Jester, D Roy, and J Post, 'Test Anxiety Effects, Predictors, and Correlates: A 30-year meta-analytic review', *Journal of Affective Disorders*, 227 (2018), 483–493

145. AJ Baxter, KM Scott, et al, 'Challenging the Myth of an "Epidemic" of Common Mental Disorders: Trends in the global prevalence of anxiety and depression between 1990 and 2010', *Depression and Anxiety*, 31/6 (2014), 506–516

146. T Heiman and K Precel, 'Students with Learning Disabilities in Higher Education: Academic strategies profile', *Journal of Learning Disabilities*, 36/3 (2003), 248–258

147. Merriam-Webster Dictionary (2020) www.merriam-webster.com /dictionary/peer%20pressure

148. 'Negative Peer Pressure: A discussion guide for adults' (Parent Further, no date) https://cnnespanol.cnn.com/wp-content /uploads/2014/11/peer_g.pdf

The Author

David C Hall is a best-selling author, motivational speaker and learning coach. He founded Potential Unlocked in 2017 and is renowned for unlocking potential in children, young people and adults.

After a childhood of special educational needs (dyslexia) that left him an 'underachiever' (four years behind his peers), David developed his own learning system that empowered him to significantly improve his academic performance and achieve GCSEs five grades above what he was predicted to attain. He has since dedicated his life and his work to unlocking young people's learning potential, improving their academic performance, helping them to find greater contentment and enjoy a passion-driven career.

David is the author of the bestselling book *The Empowering Parent* (2019) and has been invited to speak about unlocking children's and young people's potential by UK local authorities, at schools, events and seminars, and has coached adults about starting their own businesses.

Today, David works with parents, educators, policy-makers and organisations to ignite a movement of people who are fulfilled, successful and transformed, able to enjoy passion-driven careers and be positive contributors to society.

🌐 www.potentialunlocked.com
🌐 www.davidchall.co.uk
📘 www.facebook.com/DavidC.Hall1
💼 www.linkedin.com/in/davidchall1

Lightning Source UK Ltd.
Milton Keynes UK
UKHW021250111021
392014UK00011B/169